A SMALL BUSINESS AGENDA

Trends in a Global Economy

Galen Spencer Hull

UNIVERSITY
PRESS OF
AMERICA

LANHAM • NEW YORK • LONDON

Copyright © 1986 by

University Press of America,® Inc.

4720 Boston Way
Lanham, MD 20706

3 Henrietta Street
London WC2E 8LU England

Library of Congress Cataloging in Publication Data

Hull, Galen.
  A small business agenda.

  Bibliography: p.
  1. Small business—United States.   2. Small business
—Developing countries.   I. Title.
HD2346.U5H85   1986   338.6'42'0973   85-26513
ISBN 0-8191-5163-7 (alk paper)
ISBN 0-8191-5164-5 (pbk. : alk. paper)

All University Press of America books are produced on acid-free
paper which exceeds the minimum standards set by the National
Historical Publications and Records Commission.

To the memory of my mother,

Vera Mae Beighle Hull

A Small Business Agenda:

Trends in a Global Economy

Table of Contents

v

Acknowledgments

A Small Business Agenda came about as a result of several years of teaching, conducting research, and working as a consultant in developing countries. During the past ten years I have lived in the Washington, D.C., area and worked as a free lance consultant as well as for a small consulting firm which provides professional technical assistance to development agencies. My awareness of and appreciation for the role of small business has thus grown out of observations in the Third World and participation in a new and expanding small company in the United States.

Inspiration for this book was primarily derived from talking to young entrepreneurs in Africa, Asia, and the Caribbean, frequently struggling against overwhelming odds to make their mark. Most were engaged in quite mundane enterprises, operating within the "informal" sector. Some, on the other hand, viewed themselves as the vanguard of a new movement in economic development. I have also been struck by the number of government officials who readily acknowledge the need to devise new approaches to development aimed at stimulating the private sector. In the United States, one cannot help but observe the dynamic role of new and small enterprises in the economy.

I would like to acknowledge a debt of gratitude to the following persons for their moral support and assistance in bringing this manuscript to fruition: Guy Gran, Frances Johnson and Bob Palmeri were most helpful in the early stages of the project in directing me to sources of information and shaping themes. Omar Makalou and Roger Landrum read drafts of the manuscript and provided very helpful suggestions. My wife, Dawn Kepets Hull, contributed her valuable editorial assistance. Ray and Sharon Fields helped formulate the cover design and the title. Special thanks go to Sharon for her creative effort in designing the cover. Nga-Ambun Kabwasa, Rifat Barokas, and Bill Owen have also provided me with inspiration and encouragement, each in his own way.

September, 1985   Galen Spencer Hull
Kensington, Maryland

Preface

At a time when we are witnessing an increasing number of corporate mergers among the larger companies in the industrialized world, it is refreshing to come across practical ideas about fueling the steady growth of new and small businesses. In this book on small business trends in both the developed and developing countries, Galen Hull has used an approach that carries positive implications for less developed countries searching for new approaches to development.

Hull begins by giving the reader an overview of the global economy and the role of small business, surveying the current literature. He traces the historical notions of entrepreneurship from Schumpeter's classical work to contemporary writers concerned with the development process in the Third World. This leads to an examination of the fundamental problem of how to achieve a more equitable distribution of the world's scarce resources within and among countries. This has become one of the key elements of reflection after nearly forty years of international development assistance.

More recently, the relapse in the economic growth of many developing countries and the emergence of the debt crisis has forced policy-makers to rethink the modalities of development assistance. Concessional financial flows to these countries from bilateral and multilateral sources have not in many cases reached their objectives of achieving price stability, sustained economic growth, and medium-term external balance. These goals have been hampered by such negative factors as high rates of population growth, government expenditures, and personal consumption. Bilateral and multilateral funding sources have slowed down the flow of concessional assistance and commercial banks have begun to decelerate their exposure in developing countries.

Given these trends, it is essential that alternatives to past policies be examined and that new ideas be put forward. In what remains for many of us a theoretical area, Hull has provided a useful and practical perspective. Increasingly, direct investment in the developing world is being channeled through private initiatives. It is the nature and extent of these initiatives that is of particular concern in this book.

Hull draws upon his own extensive experience in developing countries. Through his well documented description of small business and entrepreneurs in the United States as well as the Third World, Hull arrives at what he calls "a small business agenda." From his survey of the growth of the entrepreneurial sector in the United States, including innovative local level initiatives and lessons learned from Europe, Hull is led to a review of proposals for development assistance. For example, he describes ideas for wholesaling capital for small enterprises, channeling blocked funds of multinational corporations toward development goals, and creating an international poverty bank.

A Small Business Agenda concludes with a summary of some practical examples of how productive energies in developing countries are being tapped without the involvement or assistance from government agencies. There is the Easy Toilet Society in India, the Al-Roadhah weavers in South Yemen, and the Retladira Welding Works in South Africa. It would appear that there is much to be learned from studying examples such as these on a case by case basis in order to understand more about how technology is transferred and how capital flows can be put to productive use. Galen Hull is to be commended for his pioneering work in this field. His book should be read by all those concerned with problems of development and with international cooperation.

Bethesda, Maryland   Omar B. Makalou
                                            Senior Advisor
September 1985   IMF Institute

Chapter One

The Global Economy and Small Business

"The United States now faces the challenge of leading the world to a new era of prosperity created...by unleashing the dynamism of the private sector in the Third World."

- The President's Task Force on International Private Enterprise, 1984

We often hear it said these days that small business is the backbone of the American economy. Yet, in an age of giant multinational corporations whose operations span the globe, it is easy to forget about the small business origins of the American society. This is especially so when the view is from a developing country. To many people in the Third World the image of the United States is shaped to a large extent by the presence of big American companies and their affiliates. Sometimes the large corporations are seen as instruments of oppression, or at least as being unmindful of the development needs of the countries in which they operate. The most frightening illustration of this was the explosion of a pesticide plant of an American owned company in India which killed hundreds of people and left many others homeless.

At the same time it is being argued that we are engaged in an ideological struggle for the minds of those living in developing countries. Conservative ideologues such as Simon Kirkpatrick, William Simon, writers such as Michael Novak and Irving Kristol (author of Two Cheers for Capitalism) are pushing for a more pro business climate in the United States, flexing their muscles in the public policy arena. Conservative think tanks, legal institutes, and academic centers funded with tens of millions of dollars from large corporations are arguing for a vastly reduced role of government in the nation's economy. They contend that the private sector should be the arbiter of the direction of the economy. Many corporate leaders now consider foreign policy questions - both economic and political - to be of paramount importance.

This "war of ideas" is being bankrolled by such groups as the John M. Olin Foundation, which has funded chairs in economics and law at a dozen universities and think tanks such as the

1

American Enterprise Institute and the Heritage Foundation. In 1978, Olin launched a clearinghouse for corporate philanthropy called the Institute for Educational Affairs (IEA). Conceived of by the head of the Olin board of trustees, William Simon, and Irving Kristol, the institute has linked conservative thinkers in need of funds with like-minded business executives. Kristol and others view power as the arbiter in international relations. They are concerned with confronting the perceived Soviet threat with force wherever necessary. Michael Novak, for example, moved beyond scholarship to lead a private-sector drive to raise money for the contra guerrillas in Nicaragua. The institute's thinkers and business leaders "share a determination to prevent our system's collapse into utter confusion."

Olin is now funding more foreign policy research than in the past, in the belief that it is now a hot topic with the troubled Western alliance. International trade issues are another of Olin's growing concerns. A recent study entitled "Policing the Global Economy: A Threat to Private Enterprise", for example, examined how a proposed United Nations code of conduct for multinationals may be hurting investment trade. Indeed, international trade has become a topic of increasing concern to many Americans, as the overvalued U.S. dollar continues to turn the United States into an international debtor nation.

If the United States is to find its way out of the current dilemma and win this "war of ideas" it must keep its small business roots uppermost in mind. If we are to achieve sustained economic growth with equity at home we must look to the entrepreneurial sector. If we are to serve as a model of development for Third World countries, it can only be through the promotion of small and medium sized enterprises, both at home and abroad. We must articulate and seek ways of implementing a small business agenda. The present inequities in the international political and economic order will only be exacerbated by following the agenda prescribed by the conservative think tanks. Their strategy of expanding the role of U.S. multinationals in international trade might lead to winning the battle against the allegedly "mercantilist" industrial powers, but it would very likely lead to losing the war of ideas among the developing nations on the periphery of the world market.

Public debate on both domestic and foreign policy issues should be focused on how best to stimulate the entrepreneurial sector of the American economy as well as the private sector in developing countries, including the "informal" sector where the vast majority of people in the Third World struggle to earn a living. The businesses of the poor, which are coming to be known as "micro-enterprises," because of their extremely small size and minimal capital investment, are too important an economic force

2

to be ignored. Even though we know little about how this informal sector operates, it is a fact that it accounts for up to 70 percent of the labor force in many developing countries.

There are several members of Congress, both liberals and conservatives, who have begun legislative initiatives designed to encourage small businesses in our own economy. As of this writing, it is too early to tell what the prospects are for these proposals. A small business political and legislative agenda in the state houses may have a better possibility of having an impact than at the national level. Those interested in reshaping foreign development assistance policy should examine these domestic initiatives and look for ways to stimulate small and medium-sized enterprises in the developing countries. By the same token, supporters of small business in the United States should be enlisted in the efforts to promote small businesses abroad, while looking for mechanisms to increase their own role in international trade.

The United States in the Global Economy

The American economy is undergoing some fundamental transformations. One of these has to do with the shift from an insular national economy to an interdependent global economy. This change is having direct consequences at home. By the beginning of 1985 a flood of imports drawn into the United States by the strong dollar completely overwhelmed the best export performance in more than three years. January's $19.4 billion in exports were the highest since September 1981. But, according to the Commerce Department, the merchandise trade deficit rose to $10.3 billion. The increasing deficit led to predictions that the continued strength of the dollar and a robust American economy would add up to continued splashes of red ink. Most analysts foresaw a trade deficit in 1985 surpassing the 1984 record of $123.3 billion.

While the flow of cheap imports was helping to dampen inflationary trends, it was also undercutting the sales of American manufacturers in their home market and holding down the rate of economic growth. Once again, the United States ran up its largest deficit with Japan - $3.7 billion - which on an annual basis would increase the 1984 record of $36.8 billion with that nation to $44.4 billion. Trade deficits with Western Europe, Taiwan, and the OPEC nations also increased in January 1985 over the previous month, while only the deficit with Canada declined. Leading imports were telecommunications equipment, passenger cars, airplanes and iron and steel products.

3

It is estimated that three-quarters of all of U.S. products are exposed to international competitive pressures. And the United States is losing relatively high-wage industrial jobs to newly industrializing countries such as Taiwan, Hong Hong, South Korea, and Singapore, countries we have been accustomed to calling Third World nations. There is a growing awareness that the global economy is somehow related to the chronic high rates of unemployment. From a modest rate of only two percent during the 1950s, the unemployment rate rose to a peak of nearly 11 percent in 1982, leveling off at around eight percent in 1985. This is the highest plateau since the Great Depression.

In April 1985, the leaders of seven industrial nations met in Bonn, West Germany, to confront trends in the global economy, including the increased tension between Japan and its trading partners and the overvalued U.S. dollar. The heads of state represented nations with a total of 22 million unemployed persons. They were all concerned about a possible downturn in the American economy that would drag the other industrial nations down with it.

Such a knowledgeable personage as the former chancellor of West Germany, Helmut Schmidt, judged this eleventh economic summit of the industrial powers to have been the least successful. In the first place, Schmidt noted that neither the Europeans nor the Japanese seemed able to adopt policies to help offset a decline in the American economy. The Reagan administration's effort to cut the budget deficit for 1986 would make some sort of slowdown in the U.S. economy inevitable. A parallel decline in the purchase of Japanese, European and Third World exports in the United States could destabilize those economies as well. Secondly, there was little significant discussion about the key economic problem in the world: the overvalued U.S. dollar brought on by the budget deficit and high interest rates. And thirdly, according to Schmidt, no agreement was reached on fighting protective tariffs and heading off trade wars by setting a date to revise the General Agreements on Trade and Tariffs (GATT).

The pressure on the United States to reduce its deficits and become more competitive in international markets has led to some rather disturbing developments. By some estimates, the dollar's long climb has cost the United States two million jobs. The strong dollar has prompted U.S. firms to transfer their production overseas. The logic of producing abroad is compelling for multinationals who sell their products around the world. While other countries flood the United States with their exports, the United States is exporting its manufacturing base and its potential economic growth. A Wall Street Journal article (April 9, 1985) illustrated this trend with some of the following examples:

4

● Tractors that Ford Motor Company has been producing in Michigan will be made at Ford plants in England and Belgium. Ford will cut 230 employees at its Michigan plant.

● Du Pont unveiled plans to expand or build new plants in Britain, France, the Netherlands, and West Germany. In March 1985, Du Pont testified in Congress that it would probably cut more jobs and production in the United States because of the strong dollar.

● Ingersoll-Rand will lay off 234 workers when it closes its New York state iron foundry; the castings made at the plant can be brought for half as much overseas.

● Goodyear Tire and Rubber has given up trying to export certain big tires for earthmovers to the Far East. Instead, it has taken a 30 percent interest in Japan's Toyo Tire Company, which will make the tires for Goodyear in Japan.

U.S. firms are making goods abroad, not only for international markets but also for sale in the United States, a tactic common in the electronics industry. Manufacturers also say that more of what goes into the goods they sell in the United States is made abroad. This foreign sourcing produces a ripple effect of lost jobs and production in the United States.

The strong dollar has had an adverse effect on smaller U.S. firms trying to operate abroad since they lack the flexibility to move production abroad. According to the Wall Street Journal article, the managing director in Britain for a Virginia-based manufacturer of heating equipment stated flatly: "We 've lost a large chunk of our business due to the dollar. We don't stand a cat-in-hell's chance; the price of U.S.-made goods is too damn high." Although the company continues to manufacture in the United States, it has begun buying parts for some of its products in Europe, shipping them to the U.S. for production, and then shipping them back to Europe for sale - all for less than it would cost to use U.S. parts. "It's all one big move away from the United States," he says.

This trend has occasioned some rather heated political comment in the United States. Sen. Lloyd Bentsen (D-Texas) charged in a letter to President Reagan that the Commerce Department is encouraging American manufacturers to move their plants overseas to become more competitive. His letter decried what seemed to be U.S. government policy, stating that "the transfer of manufacturing capacity abroad should not even be regarded benignly, let alone encouraged." The trend, he noted, is contrary to national interest because re-establishing similar activities in the United States in the future would be prohibitively expensive.

The global economy has had some rather unexpected consequences for U.S. companies operating in the Third World. In
Latin America especially, the debt crisis has forced governments
to attempt to seal themselves off from the rest of the world. In
an effort to achieve balance-of-payments surpluses in order to
pay those debts, governments have tightened up on import licences
and currency controls to slash imports and encourage exports.
This has added to the problems of the subsidiaries of U.S. companies, struggling to cope with soaring inflation rates and weak
demand. The parent companies are faced with an interruption in
the flow of profits and dividends from their subsidiaries. While
Third World governments have traditionally placed limits and
taxes on remittances, recently they have become prohibitive in
some Latin countries. This has resulted in many corporations
having blocked funds in those countries.

There are several alternatives for the disposition of these
blocked funds: corporations can simply wait out the current
situation, hoping that local assets will not be too eroded by
inflation; they can try to get the funds out of the country; or
they can use the funds locally. The first option is often the
least satisfactory. The central bank has no incentive to release
the funds, prefering to see hard currency remain in country. Some
companies resort to dubious means of getting funds out of the
country, but multinationals have too much visibility to get away
with these tactics. There are a variety of legitimate ways of
moving the blocked funds, but most of them involve complications.
So many companies are forced to find ways of using their blocked
funds locally.

Some of the methods employed to use up funds in-country involve doing business through local subsidiaries. Salesmen may be
offered vacation prizes such as a trip to Mexico or Brazil.
Equipment may be purchased locally. But most U.S. corporations
resigned to using blocked funds locally apply them to financial
investments rather than productive ones. One of the more popular
investments is in real estate. For example, Volkswagen has acquired ranches in the interior of Brazil and Xerox owns one of
the largest buildings in Bogota. Latin American governments
have been hoping that the multinationals would use blocked funds
to enter into joint ventures with local enterprises. But given
the usual government regulations and shrinking Latin American
markets, few U.S. firms have been willing to go that route.

Some observers suggest that one of the more hopeful signs
for the economic future of Latin America is that a few companies
are beginning to use their cash to generate additional export
earnings. Firms that originally went into Brazil or Mexico to ex-
ploit the domestic market view those countries less as a market
than an export platform, which coincides with government inten-
tions in the first place. Ford, for example, plans to locate a

big share of its truck manufacturing in Brazil and is expanding local production of automobile components.

The Third World and the International Market

The international trade war has brought about some developments that have tested the ideological integrity of capitalists and socialists alike. A group of U.S. corporations, lured by the potential for capitalist profits in officially Marxist Mozambique, have taken advantage of a Reagan administration policy intended to bolster that nation's sagging economy. Former Defense Secretary Melvin Laird headed a trade mission consisting of representatives from Tenneco, Teledyne, and other companies, and sponsored by the U.S. government to the southern African nation. The idea was endorsed by the administration in order to show Mozambique the benefits of the private sector. The mission, however, was bitterly criticized by some New Right activists who see a fundamental contradiction in promoting such trade. They argue that Mozambique is no different from Nicaragua in that both nations are headed by Marxist regimes fighting pro-Western guerrilla insurgencies. While the administration imposed a trade embargo barring U.S. companies from doing business in Nicaragua, its policy in Mozambique is just the opposite: offering economic and military aid and encouraging American corporations to invest.

Howard Phillips, chairman of the Conservative Caucus, charged that this policy "is particularly shameful for this administration, given its rhetoric on behalf of freedom fighters." He remarked that this illustrated the basic split in the Republican Party between "those who support freedom and those who are guided by the profit motive." For their part, State Department officials made no bones about the fact they wanted to see U.S. companies return to Mozambique for the first time since the country became independent in 1975. They justified the new initiative on the basis of international geopolitics and internal changes within Mozambique itself. President Samora Machel in recent months had shown growing disenchantment with the Soviets who had befriended Mozambique since independence. He had joined the World Bank, submitted Mozambique's books to the International Monetary Fund, and exchanged ambassadors with the United States.

Numerous developing countries that embraced socialism at independence have also been experimenting with private sector initiatives. One of the most eloquent spokesmen of African socialism has been President Julius Nyerere of Tanzania. The program of self reliance which he launched in the late 1960s was

7

aimed at achieving economic independence while avoiding the class
conflict usually attendent upon capitalist development. The
socialist principles set forth sought to keep traditional commu-
nal values intact and at the same time create an industrial
economy with government as the primary engine of development.

By 1985, after several years of stagnation in the Tanzanian
economy, President Nyerere announced the lifting of his nation's
14-year ban on private ownership of rental housing. He also made
public a plan to sell off many state-owned farming estates to
private business people. Tanzanians do not necessarily concede
that they are abandoning socialist development. Finance Minister
Cleopa Msuya, the official most responsible for overseeing policy
reforms, put it this way: "Cutting costs is neither socialism nor
capitalism; it's just common sense."

Socialist-oriented countries such as Tanzania, Ethiopia,
Zambia, and Mozambique have expended considerable efforts on
education for development. And in many cases they have in fact
dramatically increased the literacy rates of their population.
Some have been successful at improving other social services as
well. But, like other African countries that chose to follow a
more mixed economy development policy, they have found it increasingly difficult to provide for the basic needs of their people. To some extent their attempts to introduce market mechanisms into their economies is due to pressure from western
donors and lenders such as the World Bank and the International
Monetary Fund. But there is also evidence to indicate that African political leaders recognize the need to promote small and
medium sized enterprises, having seen their dreams of rapid
industrial growth through large state-owned enterprises dashed.

The transformation under way in the People's Republic of
China is even more notable, if only because Chairman Mao's revolutionary socialism served as inspiration for would-be revolu-
tionaries around the world. Mao's successor, Deng Xiaoping, is
fashioning a far more pragmatic approach to development, without
renouncing socialism. His policy is one of "building socialism
with capitalist methods." Deng's major pronouncements are included in a pamphlet entitled Building China with Socialist
Characteristics. It emphasizes productivity as the solution to
the country's economic and social needs. The policies aim at
transforming a centrally planned economy into a more market-
oriented one. The objective is to quadruple the value of industrial and agricultural output by the year 2000.

Deng's reforms began in the countryside shortly after he
came to power in 1979. He made agriculture the first priority of
his "four modernization" plans, with industry, science, and
defense following in that order. The new "responsibility" system
provided incentives to farmers: once they turned over their quota

8

of crops to the government, they were free to sell the rest on the open market. The prices which the government pays for these quotas were also raised. This is by no means a return to agricultural capitalism since the land is still legally owned collectively. However, under the new system farmers sign contracts for both land and equipment and use them at their discretion, thus giving them more of a sense of proprietorship. These innovations have proven successful: grain harvest rose to a record 400 million tons in 1984 while the average farmer's income doubled.

But the boom did not extend to the urban areas, where most of the state-owned enterprises are located. Then, in October 1984, Deng moved to apply a package of reforms aimed at stimulating the urban economy and providing incentives to industrial workers. The program called for cutting back on central planning and giving most state-owned enterprises autonomy to vary prices they charge. This involved removing government subsidies which accounted for a large portion of the nation's budget and allowing prices to respond to market forces. Many Chinese feared that the cost of such basic items as rice and clothes would soar as a result of these measures. The hardest hit would be the 80 million urban workers.

The implications of the reforms for small business are considerable. The growing number of businesses owned by individuals and small groups should be able to offer their goods at whatever price the market will stand. The government planners will likely see their powers of regulation reduced. They will have a decreased power over prices to guide the economy and will have to learn to use taxes instead. The big subsidies on basic materials will gradually be cut, and prices will rise to meet demand. This in turn will likely lead to inflation as incomes for some increase.

Clearly these reforms represent a big gamble for Deng Xiaoping and his pragmatic leadership. Some members of the Politburo have strong reservations about the reforms because of their capitalistic tendencies. The policies will likely increase the gap between rich and poor, and between the developing coastal area and the backward interior. They will raise the likelihood of unemployment as a result of a massive drift of population from the villages into the towns in search of jobs. Some argue that these are bold reforms which could mark an important schism in the communist world, leaving the Soviet Union alone in its attempt to follow Leninist orthodoxy.

The implications of the modernization program launched by Deng are considerable for the West. In his speech to the Central Advisory Commission in October 1984, Deng remarked that, "no country can now develop by closing its door." He was defending

9

his policy of building ties to the West. "We sufferred from this, and our forefathers suffered from this. Isolation landed China in poverty, backwardness and ignorance." He argued that only through foreign investment and trade could China achieve its goal of quadrupling its gross national product to $1 trillion by the year 2000.

Just as observers were applauding the Chinese opening to the West, Deng demonstrated his penchant for pragmatism by arranging an agreement with the Soviet Union to boost bilateral trade over the next five years. The $14 billion pact appeared to indicate continued improvement in relations between the two communist giants. Despite continuing political differences, Moscow and Peking moved a long way since deciding to normalize their relations in the fall of 1982. According to the terms of the agreement the Soviets will help modernize China's industry by supplying machinery, machine-tool equipment, chemicals, cars and trucks, and raw materials. Chinese deliveries to the Soviets will consist of consumer goods, agricultural commodities, and some raw materials. Since Chinese agricultural production has increased sharply they have been looking for food export markets.

America II and the Entrepreneurial Revolution

According to journalist Richard Louv, the America we know is dying, but a second America is rising from the body of the first. In his book, America II, Mr. Louv characterizes America I as consisting of decaying urban centers, labor unions, New Deal politics, public services, smokestack industries, and free-standing single-family homes. The second America? High tech industries, home-based entrepreneurs, electronic mailboxes, and planned condominium communities, all evolving in an information revolution.

The engine for the development of America II is small business, fueled by a renewed spirit of entrepreneurialism. It serves as an escape clause in the post-industrial economy. Until the 1980s, small business enjoyed no particular distinction. Now, in a period of insecurity, it's the new faith. This is of course ironic because starting a new business is among the most insecure of endeavors. The new entrepreneurs, however, see this as an alternative to a traditional job market that leaves little room for flexibility. People take all the energy they used to put into "est" or whatver and pour it into their businesses. Louv even suggests that entrepreneurialism is a kind of new religion, come to replace the social activism of the 1960s and the human potential movement and psychotherapy of the 1970s.

10

In fact, so many people are calling themselves entrepreneurs these days that the meaning of the word has become hazy. The classical definition of the entrepreneur was an innovative capitalist, as distinguished from a garden-variety capitalist who used other people's innovations to make money. The basic ingredient still seems to be the willingness to take a risk for the sake of profit. Common wisdom used to hold that companies, like cities, would grow and grow, and that small businesses would eventually fade into insignificance. Some noted economists were predicting in the 1950s that the entrepreneur would disappear, swept away by the advantages inherent in large corporate organization and capitalization. But by the 1980s there were more than 600,000 new businesses being created each year, compared with only 93,000 in 1950. It must be added that the death rate for new businesses is also higher now.

Why did entrepreneurialism begin to expand, even in the worst recession since the 1930s? Louv summarizes a few reasons:

● It accords with the trend away from a manufacturing economy toward a service/information economy. Generally it takes less capital investment to set up shop in an information or service business than in a manufacturing plant.

● Population deconcentration is both a stimulant and a result of the new entrepreneurialism. The Southwest, with its looser zoning regulations and lower taxes, is more attuned to the entrepreneur.

● The trend away from mass-produced goods and a shift toward individual goods and services is also stimulating the growth of entrepreneurialism. Money now being spent on mass-produced goods will likely shift toward specialized crafts and personalized products of cottage industries.

● The two-paycheck family is also influencing the entrepreneurial movement. In a family with two incomes, there is a better possibility that one spouse can take the risk involved in setting up a new business.

● Entrepreneurialism is a pressure-release valve in an economy that has less and less room for middle managers because of the new computer technology. There just isn't room enough for all the baby boomers who want to be executives.

● The easiest way to become an entrepreneur is to work out of the home. As many as 5 million people may be working out of their own homes, and the number is growing.

11

Against all these factors stimulating the entrepreneurial boom must be weighed others not so positive. The new movement creates resentment to government regulation among those who in the past were idealistic about what government should do for the common good. Then, too, the same forces propelling the growth of tax-paying independent contractors is also fueling another kind of growth: going underground. The IRS estimates that upwards of $300 billion in income in 1981 went unreported. This underground cash economy is growing twice as fast as the gross national product.

Louv is not entirely sanguine about America II. He sees the nation fragmenting into subsocieties, regions, sections, and information-rich versus information-poor, rather than defining what we want: security, economic stability, and community. Americans are moving into new tribes, into condo communities and urban villages. The selectivity of these new tribes ultimately means that a few members have the key to the future. The new tribes work wonderfully for those who can afford them, through money or knowledge.

Louv would like to see a third vision emerge which would suggest that smaller governments and entrepreneurial enterprises are good for the nation. It would encourage small farms and discourage the privatization of public responsibility. It would include federal assistance to help people move to jobs and massive training programs to ease those shoved out or left behind by the new economy, not only into high-tech jobs, but into entrepreneurial endeavors. The third vision would provide a sense of national purpose that would be healing. Down this road we would form stronger and more lasting bonds of family and friendship instead of walled enclaves.

Small Business and the Entrepreneur

Small business and entrepreneurship are terms that are often mentioned in the same breath. Students of development have struggled with their definitions for a long time. Raymond Brown has explored the dimensions of entrepreneurship and development in a doctoral dissertation. In his survey of the growing literature on the subject, Brown points out that Joseph Schumpeter devoted considerable attention to the concept of the entrepreneur in development. He saw the entrepreneur as first and foremost an "innovator" who "carries out new combinations", thus providing the driving force in economic development. An encylopedic definition of entrepreneurship has come to include "purposeful, successful activity to initiate, maintain, or develop a profit-oriented business..." It is often associated with risk taking in economic development.

12

Some writers such as Albert Shapero have argued for a broader interpretation of entrepreneurship to include creative, initiative-taking activities that fall outside of company formations. He maintains that even the creation of a community theatre group or an independent government organization could be considered an "entrepreneurial event." The key role of the entrepreneur is to organize and mobilize productive resources, assuming the risk of loss or failure in a changing and uncertain environment.

E.F. Schumacher, who popularized the idea of small business development in his book Small is Beautiful in 1973, championed it as a unique institution, not merely a replica of big business. For Schumacher, the small size requisite is the imperative condition. He requires the enterprize to be "local" so as to curb its expansion. The business has to be personal, in the familial paternal sense. Ownership of property is linked to creative work. In sum, Schumacher's small business is a hybrid derived from contradictions in both capitalist and socialist economic traditions. Even though his small business is under capitalist sponsorship, it has more in common with small businesses in the People's Republic of China under Mao than those of the U.S. or Great Britain.

Schumacher's small business manifesto is summed up in his discussion of ownership:

● In small-scale enterprise, private ownership is natural, fruitful and just;

● In medium-scale enterprise, private ownership is already to a large extent functionally unnecessary. The idea of property becomes strained, unfruitful, and unjust;

● In large-scale enterprise, private ownership is a fiction for the purpose of enabling functionless owners to live parasitically on the labor of others.

Schumacher was something of a voice crying in the wilderness in the United States during the 1970s, except among those who were involved in experiments in small enterprise development in the Third World. But by 1985, even the American business establishment had taken up the refrain. The May 27 issue of Business Week boldly proclaimed that "Small is Beautiful."

Indeed, entrepreneurship has become a popular item in the media. The staid Wall Street Journal weighed in with a special report on small business and entrepreneurs. Best-selling books such as Megatrends, The Third Wave, and In Search of Excellence

13

underscored the trends toward self-employment, risk-taking, and bottom-up initiatives in the business world. Business schools began offering special programs in entrepreneurial studies and seminars for business executives to hone their entrepreneurial skills. In his speech defending the administration's tax reforms President Reagan proclaimed this the Age of the Entrepreneur.

Statistics tend to substantiate the claim that the small business sector in the United States is providing the cutting edge of economic recovery. The President's report on the State of Small Business published in May 1985 revealed some interesting facts:

● From October 1982 through October 1984, employment in industries dominated by small firms rose 11.4 percent, while employment industries dominated by large businesses rose only 5.3 percent.

● Small business income, as measured by sole proprietorships and partnerships, increased 33.7 percent during the first six months of 1984. The small business income gain in 1983 was 11.3 percent.

● In 1984 new business incorporations totaled approximately 640,000, a new record. The revious record of 600,000 was set in 1983. Business starts during the first half of 1984 increased by seven percent.

● Women-owned businesses are the fastest growing part of the small business population. From 1977 to 1982, the number of women-owned sole proprietorships increased at an annual rate of 6.9 percent, while all sole proprietorships increased at an annual rate of only 3.7 percent. About one in every four sole proprietorships is owned by a woman.

● Women operate three million of the 14.2 million non-farm small businesses in the United States.

● Small businesses continue to pay interest rates at a premium of two to three percent, compared to rates paid by large firms. However, equity financing for young and fast-growing firms has increased dramatically during the last several years.

● Small businesses offer less comprehensive fringe benefits to their employees than do large corporations. This gap has not narrowed in recent years, making it harder for small businesses to attract and retain a quality work force. The main reason for the continuing gap is the relatively lower profit margins of small firms.

14

Small Business in the Third World

We are not accustomed to thinking of small business in the Third World as being in any respect similar to those in the industrialized countries. The role of small business in the development process has been the subject of numerous studies over the past 30 years. The sector has come to be commonly known as small and medium-scale enterprises (SME). The scale of operations is generally defined in terms of the number of employees. Those industries with 100 or more employees are considered to be large-scale, compared with 500 or more in the United States. Medium-scale industries are those with 50 to 99 employees. Small-scale industries are defined as having between 10 and 49 employess, while household or cottage industries are those with fewer than 10. The latter are also referred to as micro-enterprises.

It is frequently noted that we still know little about the actual performance of these household or cottage enterprises in the developing world. However, small and medium-scale industries are generally considered to play an important role in both income generation and employment creation. These "informal" types of enterprises account for a very substantial portion of employment in Third World countries. The "underground economy" in Peru, for example, is estimated to absorb as much as 60 percent of the workforce and to provide 85 percent of internal transportation. In Lima alone, with a population of 5,500,000, micro-enterprises number between 300,000 and 500,000, and represent between 30 and 70 percent of the labor force.

As in the economies of the industrial countries, these small enterprises are considered to have several positive features:

● Small and medium-scale businesses are labor-intensive and use relatively simple techniques of production, which correspond with the abundance of labor and scarcity of capital in most developing countries;

● They provide an especially large share of the jobs available to women, recent immigrants from rural areas, and youth;

● They provide goods and services to the poor in small quantities which meet basic needs - half an onion, shoes, school uniforms - at low cost and often on credit;

● They are considered more efficient in the use of capital and in mobilizing savings, entrepreneurial talent, and other resources that would otherwise not be tapped; a typical shoemaker

15

has ten years of experience as an apprentice and master crafts-
man before opening a small shop;

● They provide a vital link to modern enterprises, distri-
buting their products and producing finished goods for resale and
export;

● Small businesses sometimes succeed by serving limited or
specialized markets that are not attractive to larger industries.

At the same time, small businesses in the developing world
face obstacles seemingly more overwhelming than those in the
industrialized countries:

● They face very limited access to institutional credit from
banks and other lending institutions;

● They lack technical and marketing assistance, often depending upon traditional moneylenders who charge rates ranging
from 20 percent a month to 20 percent a day in most countries;

● They are confronted with a hostile policy environment -
administrative controls on interest rates, tariffs and investment
incentives favoring large firms, and agricultural policies which
inhibit the growth of rural incomes - that considers them to be
essentially outside of the law;

● They lack access to the raw materials and other advantages of larger businesses.

Nonetheless, there is a growing recognition among politicians and scholars alike that the small enterprise sector represents tremendous potential for development. Some governments are
well advanced in devising policies that are intended to stimulate
the growth of these enterprises. Most international donor
agencies and many private voluntary organizations are attempting
to learn more about how the informal sector works. And they are
beginning to provide resources aimed at making these enterprises
self sustaining rather than depending upon government welfare.

U.S. Development Assistance to Developing Countries

Traditionally programs of development assistance, whether
bilateral or multilateral, have been aimed at building the capabilities of government institutions. In the past decade these
have typically taken the form of large integrated rural development projects with several components, whose recurrent costs the
host government is unable to sustain. The Third World is strewn
with white elephants of this sort.

16

In recent years the private sector in developing countries has been re-discovered by students of development and policy planners, as well as politicians. For example, the World Bank charted its course of action in Africa for the 1980s with the oft quoted Accelerated Development in Sub-Saharan Africa, published in 1981. Surveying the economic crisis on the continent, the report concluded that a gloomy future lay ahead unless certain policy changes and structural adjustments were made. Among other recommendations, it urged the promotion of indigenous African enterprises through policy changes. And it projected an increase in investment opportunites for foreign companies with the revival of the minerals market during the 1980s.

Early in the first Reagan administration, an AID policy paper stated that greater reliance on private enterprise in Third World development would be essential to the achievement of AID objectives. It maintained that the poor performance of low income countries could be attributed to government policies that have inhibited market incentives. AID set up a new Private Enterprise Bureau (PRE) to pursue the goal of a private sector initiative to foster the growth of a productive, self sustaining income and job producing private sector in developing countries. Private sector development became the centerpiece of the administration's development assistance policy.

In May 1983 the President established a task force on international private enterprise to examine how U.S. foreign assistance could be used to promote investment in and trade with developing countries. In December 1984 the President's task force published its findings, which included a recommendation that AID's legislative mandate as well as its resource availability and organizational structure be revised to reflect a greater private sector emphasis. It also recommended that AID serve more as a broker between U.S. businesses and prospective overseas partners by providing information on the investment climate and conditions in developing countries.

The indigenous enterprises that have been the target of U.S. development assistance are often as not the larger ones. The task force catalogued in a second volume guidebook the various tools available to U.S. officials for promoting private enterprise. For example, financing of intermediate credit institutions (ICIs) has been a major instrument for assisting capital market development. Since the 1960s AID has used this approach to further such objectives as broadening access to the formal credit system and developing institutional capability for appraisal banking. There has been a tendency for the ICI loans to be directed at larger and better established enterprises. Small firms have received little attention because of their high risk nature.

17

The Entente Fund's African Enterprise Program, for example, was provided ICI assistance to be made available to national development banks in five West African member countries. An evaluation of the program indicated that larger firms were generally favored over the small ones and that inside contacts were typically used to obtain funds.

This is not to say that small and medium-sized enterprises have been entirely overlooked in U.S. development assistance programs. In recent years there have been some notable attempts within AID to experiment with projects aimed at assisting the small enterprise sector. In 1978, the Office of Urban Development initiated a project which came to be known by the acronym PISCES: Program for Investment in the Small Capital Enterprise Sector. Its purpose was to improve AID's understanding of the nature and constraints of the sector, and to eventually upgrade its ability to design projects which promote employment among the poor. In the first two phases of the project, surveys were conducted on the role of small, labor-intensive enterprises, and methodologies were developed for evaluating their impact.

In the third phase, AID contracted with three private voluntary organizations to help develop and implement small enterprise projects in urban areas of selected countries. Two of these, ACCION International and Partnership for Productivity, had been providing small loans and technical assistance to small enterprises in developing countries for several years. A third organization, the Development Group for Alternative Policies, was a strong advocate for public policies promoting small enterprise. Findings from four regional case studies of the first phase of the PISCES project were compiled in a published volume in 1981. Some of the programs assisted sizeable numbers of businesses with initial loans ranging from $12 to $300. Administrative costs were relatively low, and payback rates ranged as high as 90 to 99 percent. Other projects helped small-scale entrepreneurs enter urban activities such as selling prepared food. Research under the PISCES project showed that it was possible to train poor youths in higher paying skills and help them start their own new businesses or cooperatives in which resources were pooled.

There are other examples of discrete efforts aimed at small and medium-scale enterprises which receive some form of official U.S. development assistance. Women's World Banking (WWB) helps Third World women who do not have access to credit with formal institutuions. WWB, an independent financing institution with offices in New York, has joined local affiliates in helping women entrepreneurs obtain credit in businesses ranging from clothing shops and doll making to food vending. WWB has also assisted in buying, marketing, and business management in such countries as the Dominican Republic, Thailand, and Kenya.

The Young President's Organization (YPO), also based in New York, has involved the presidents of small and medium-sized U.S. firms in assisting managers in developing countries with practical problems. YPO is comprised of over 3,600 executives who built their companies from the ground up by the age of 40. An AID grant promotes visits by YPO teams to five targeted countries - Indonesia, Jamaica, Kenya, Sri Lanka, and Thailand - where they meet with local executives and share their experience in marketing and management.

For several years the Peace Corps has fielded a few volunteers in a wide range of projects to promote income generation. This remains a small area of Peace Corps programming, but with considerable potential for expansion. In 1985 there were a total of 5,600 volunteers worldwide, of whom only 421 were in jobs related to small business development. Many of them were involved in cooperatives and credit unions, while others provided business advisory services in accounting and business management. The largest small business programs were in the Philippines, Fiji, Micronesia, Kenya, Costa Rica, and Honduras.

Business leaders from Third World countries have been on tours sponsored by the United States Information Agency's International Visitors Program. The purpose of the program is to provide a better understanding of how the American economic system works, and in particular what factors encourage or inhibit small business development. The program examines the potential for small businesses to generate new and diverse employment opportunities. It also aims at fostering an exchange of ideas on how to stimulate small business. During the thirty-day program, participants visit states such as South Carolina which have made major strides in fostering successful small business creation.

It is not at all clear, however, that programs of international public assistance to private enterprise development in the Third World can work any better than the programs designed to assist the public sector. Indeed, some argue that even less government and international assistance is warranted. They would say that government is part of the problem, not the solution. On the other hand, it is by no means certain that a development assistance policy whose basic rationale is to make the world safe for expanded investments and exports of large U.S. corporations abroad will in any way contribute to the development needs of the Third World. For those who accept the premise that the promotion of small business development is an appropriate strategy for international development, Chapter Five provides a menu of diverse approaches - both public and private - to this objective.

Small Business and Public Policy

One of the clearest indices of the economy's ability to support its population is the rate of unemployment, which has been
growing in the United States ever since 1950. The average rate
has increased two points each decade since then, from only two
percent during the 1950s to eight percent today. Neither the
Democrats nor the Republicans have devised an economic policy to
effectively address this critical labor market trend. Some
policy-makers refer to a "natural rate of unemployment." Supply
side economists argue that unemployment will take care of itself
whenever the economic recovery takes hold. And the Keynesians
have also tended to assume that productivity will be taken care
of by businessmen, with the right macro-economic demand policies.
Both schools of thought are premised on the assumption that
private markets act perfectly, given the correct set of macro-
economic policies.

There is a new movement that argues against both of these
positions, proposing instead what is called an "entrepreneurial
policy." The Corporation for Enterprise Development (CfED) is
articulating this approach, maintaining that while an appropriate
macro-economic policy is necessary, it is not in itself
sufficient. CfED contends that markets, like all other human institutions, do not function perfectly. For example, investment
does not always flow to areas of highest return (controlling for
risk). Seed and equity investment is often unavailable to those
new and growing businesses which are creating the most new jobs
and introducing the most innovations. Investable assets, CfED
point outs, are becoming increasingly concentrated in large institutions which find it difficult and costly to make long-term
investments in small deals.

Those who espouse an entrepreneurial policy use the term
"entrepreneur" in its most catholic sense. Entrepreneurs include not only those who start independent, for-profit businesses, but non-profit enterprises as well. The latter constitute more than one-fifth of the economy and provide real value
in every sense of the word. They also include new ventures of
larger institutions, both public and private, where "intrapreneurship" is becoming fashionable. The prototype of the indivi-
dualistic white Anglo-Saxon male entrepreneur is having to make
way for a new breed of women, minorities, and disadvantaged entrepreneurs.

CfED chronicles developments within the entrepreneurial
movement. One of the major changes in the past five years has
been a shift in state economic development policy from chasing
and attracting "smokestack" industries with tax incentives and
other subsidies, to focusing on the importance of "home-growing"

one's own indigenous economy. States are now attempting to foster the formation and expansion of new, young, and small firms. Another development was the refinement of the concept of capital market failure, which has led to new measures designed to remedy them. For example, there is a new generation of risk capital-oriented state development finance vehicles such as the Massachusetts Technology Development Corporation.

At the same time there are voices in the United States being raised in support of policies that would stimulate increased exports by small businesses. The Center for the Study of Democratic Institutions in Santa Barbara, California, for example, sponsored a panel in 1984 on entrepreneurship and the dilemma of small business. Participants agreed that the biggest potential for increased U.S. exports could well come from the small businesses that do not now export or do so on a very modest scale. Small business could be an important answer to the U.S. trade deficit problem. Currently, however, small business is disadvantaged in international trade. One per cent of U.S. firms account for fully eighty per cent of exports. Only 30,000 out of 376,000 manufacturers in the United States have ever exported, even though one out of eight manufacturing jobs depends on exports.

Small businesses in the United States face a number of problems that sound remarkably similar to those faced by small businesses in the developing world. In a recent survey of chief executives of small businesses, it was discovered that the two major problems were identifying and training good employees, and dealing with government regulations. Lack of capital and access to credit institutions also pose problems. When a small business does become successful, big businesses come along to copy the product or buy the company out.

One participant proposed a worldwide free trade zone for small businesses. He referred to the basic rules for free trade set forth in the Generalized Agreement on Trade and Tariff (GATT). Under the GATT system of preferences, businesses in 140 disadvantaged countries are allowed to have free entry into our markets for over 3000 products. He argued for extending the same system to small, independently owned and operated businesses in the United States and around the world.

This is a very brief examination of the range of issues surrounding private sector development in general and small business in particular. There is still considerable debate as to what kind of public policy, if any, the United States should have to generate employment and stimulate the entrepreneurial sector. These issues are treated in more detail in the following chapters. It will be argued that we are in fact in need of policies that promote these twin objectives. An effort will be made to demonstrate that a policy of small business promotion in the United States is equally appropriate to Third World countries. A strategy of small and medium enterprise development would accord with the increased attention to policy changes in developing countries that are aimed at promoting small business. To the extent U.S. development assistance policy reflects a preoccupation with the trade deficit and only a modest concern for the development of indigenous enterprises, it is not likely to have a development impact on developing nations.

Chapter One References

AID, The President's Task Force on International Private Enterprise: Report to the President, accompanied by a second volume, The Private Enterprise Guidebook; available from AID's Center for Development Information and Evaluation, December 1984.

Peter Stone, "Businesses Widen Role in Conservatives' War of Ideas," Washington Post, May 12, 1985.

Helmut Schmidt, "The Trade War Threat," Washington Post Magazine, June 16, 1985.

Steve Gerstel, "Commerce Advice Criticized," Washington Post, June 10, 1985.

Stuart Auerbach, "U.S. Trade Deficit Climbs in January to $10.3 Billion," Washington Post, March 1, 1985.

Gary Putka, "Strong Dollar Has Led U.S. Firms to Transfer Production Overseas,", Wall Street Journal, April 9, 1985.

Michael Isikoff, "U.S. Firms Eye New Ties With Mozambique," Washington Post, May 1985.

Glenn Frankel, "Socialism Seen Losing Appeal in Africa," Washington Post, June 6, 1985.

"China Notes that Marx is Dead," The Economist, December 22, 1984.

"It Cannot Harm Us: From Merit Raises to Free-Market Prices, Deng Pushes His Daring Reforms," Time, January 14, 1985.

Henriette Sender, "What to do about Blocked Funds," in Dun's Business Month, June 1984.

Richard Louv, America II: The Book that Captures Americans in the Act of Creating the Future, New York: Penguin Books, 1983.

Raymond Brown, Indigenous Enterprises in Less Developed Countries: The Importance of Entrepreneurs to the Development Process, PhD dissertation, Clarement Graduate School, 1982.

E.F. Schumacher, Small is Beautiful: Economics as if People Mattered, New York: Harper & Row, 1973.

The State of Small Business: A Report of the President, trans-
    mitted to the Congress in May 1985; Washington, D.C.:
    Small Business Administration

Michael Farbman, (ed.) The PISCES Studies: Assisting the Small-
    est Economic Activities of the Urban Poor, AID, Office of
    Urban Development, Bureau for Science and Technology, 1981.

The Entrepreneurial Economy (editorial), "Reducing Unemployment
    Through Entrepreneurial Policy," January 1984.

"Entrepreneurship and the Dilemma of Small Business in America,"
    in The Center Magazine, a publication of the Center for the
    Study of Democratic Institutions, associated with the Univer-
    sity of California, (January/February 1985).

Chapter Two

The Entrepreneurial Economy in the United States

"...What astonished me in the United States is not so much the marvelous grandeur of some undertakings as the innumerable multitude of small ones."
                                    - Alexis de Tocqueville
                                      Democracy in America, 1835

"...The greatest innovations for new jobs, technologies and economic vigor today come from a small but growing circle of heroes - the small business people, American entrepreneurs, men and women of faith, intellect, and daring who take great risks to invest in and invent our future.'

                                    - President Reagan
                                      Address on Taxes, May 1985

Megatrends

     It has become fashionable in recent years for futurologists to echo the prescient observations of de Tocqueville on the dynamic of the American economy. In the 1950s conventional wisdom foresaw the end of the entrepreneur and the ascendency of the bureaucratic system. William H. Whyte's Organization Man described young Americans as aspiring to work for somebody else, to be technicians and collaborators in large corporations. The dream of independence through a business of one's own was held almost exclusively by factory workers.

     By the late 1970s there was an entrepreneurial boom and a corresponding trend toward self-employment. One of the first futurologists to identify this trend was Alvin Toffler, whose book Future Shock (1970) predicted the rise of risk-taking and a new entrepreneurial spirit. When he published The Third Wave (1981), Toffler was talking about the "electronic cottage" of home-based businesses. In his most recent book, Previews and Promises, (1983) Toffler examines the 350,000 home-based, women-owned businesses in the country. He sees these as a little undiscovered island in the economy, accounting for billions of dollars worth of business.

     Toffler views the mass manufacturing industries - auto, steel, rubber, and textile which have been the backbone of the economy - as being in "terminal agony." Simultaneously, we are

25

witnessing the rise of electonics, computers, information, genetics, and aerospace. What's happening, he says, is not so much a recession as a "restructuring of the entire techno-economic base of the society." The central proposition of Toffler's work is that today's crisis is not one of redistribution or of low productivity but a crisis of restructure. It is the breakdown of the old Second Wave: the industrial era economy and the emergence of a new Third Wave that operates on different principles. This involves moving from a mass production, mass consumption economy to what Toffler calls a "de-massified" economy.

Toffler argues that the restructuring also involves a change from a national to regional economies. During the age of industrialism, the United States went from small-scale enterprises serving local communities to bigger and bigger companies operating on a national scale. This was made possible by the new industrial technologies, transportation and communication systems that tied the nation together. In recent decades we have witnessed the rise of the multinational corporation. The power of technology jumped to a new stage in which the international banking system was reorganized to service giant multinational corporations. An increasingly large portion of world production was done for international rather than national markets.

At the same time this process was going on, however, little attention was being paid to the opposite trend gathering momentum: the shift from national to regional production. When we look at Texas or Quebec we find regional economies that have become as large and complex as national economies were a decade ago. These regional economies are diverging rather than converging. This means that managing them centrally from the national level - whether in Washington, Tokyo, or Moscow - will become more and more difficult. Nowadays, uniform national policies cause increasingly dangerous side effects in regional or local economies.

Another writer who has become well known for his studies of the nature of work in the American economy is David Birch, a professor at MIT. He published an article in 1979 entitled "The Job Generation Process," which launched him into a select group of futurologists whose work is widely read. Birch discovered that a large proportion of the new jobs being created in the United States were not to be found where economists and policymakers had generally looked for them. Jobs were not being created by the Fortune 500, or even 1500, but by small businesses and those that had been small only a few years ago. As Birch puts it: "I'm looking at myths...such as the myth that little companies fail the minute they open their doors and that big companies are here forever."

Birch sees two classes of small businesses: entrepreneurial and income-substitution businesses. The latter are by far the most common, constituting as they do 80 to 90 percent of all small businesses in the country. They include pizza parlors, real estate brokerages, and produce stores. They are income-substitution businesses because rather than working for a company, you work for yourself. Your purpose is not to create or grow something, but to generate an income to support the family. By contrast, the entrepreneurial businesspeople represent only 12 to 14 percent of all small businesses. They view growing a corporation as an art form. It is a way of life, as opposed to a way of making a living.

Birch takes special pains to debunk the popular notion that as much as 85 percent of all small business ventures fail. In fact, he says, the first year 20 percent of new businesses are gone, the second year another 15 percent disappear, in the third year another 10 percent, and so on. In other words, according to Birch, the chance of your failing in a new business in the United States is closer to 50 percent. It is important to learn what happens to these firms. They may have just quit, nothing lost, nothing gained. Or they might have closed out the business with a substantial gain. We do know that out of the 550,000 business closings each year, only 15,000 are bankruptcies, which Birch considers quite a success story.

Although Birch is generally considered to be "pro small business," he says that he is not necessarily anti-big business. When he reported that two-thirds of all new jobs created between 1969 and 1976 were in companies with 20 or fewer employees, he did not argue that governments should devise policies to help small companies. And when he pointed out that in 1982-1983 the Fortune 500 lost 310,000 jobs while the rest of the economy was creating 3 million, Birch did not condemn large corporations. In fact, he argues that the role of government is minimal in the performance of the system he is describing. He does predict, however, that we will have a serious wealth-distribution problem within the United States if present trends continue. A smaller percentage of the people now control more of the wealth than they did 30 to 40 years ago. It is already a serious problem between the United States and the rest of the world.

Birch has described a fundamental shift from large-scale enterprises to small-scale, and from bureaucratic to entrepreneurial styles of management. By the 1970s, companies that had fewer than 100 employees accounted for 80 percent of the new jobs, with most of the companies concentrated in the service sector. Investors in small companies have done far better than those who invested in large firms since the 1960s. A flood of venture capital is pouring into small entrepreneurial firms, especially those in electronics.

Peter Drucker, the guru of American management science, has also focused his attention on the entrepreneurial economy. He notes that Americans are at last learning how to manage entrepreneurship. It is no longer news, he says, that small and new businesses provided most of the 20 million new jobs generated from 1970 to 1980 in the American economy. The trend even accelerated during the recent recession. While Fortune 500 companies were losing three million jobs over the past three years, businesses less than 10 years old have added at least 750,000 jobs. Drucker points out that, contrary to popular assumptions, high-tech companies account for only a small portion of the entrepreneurial sector. Of the 100 fastest-growing publicly owned firms, only one quarter are computer-related.

Drucker outlines most of the same factors that have led to the emergence of the entrepreneurial economy described above. But he adds that the most important factor is that American industry has begun to learn how to manage entrepreneurship. Many of the new entrepreneurs have learned what almost none of their predecessors knew: why and how to manage. In fact, the very businesses they are in often involve the application of systematic management. Drucker gives the example of a barbershop business in the Southwest. Traditionally barbershops were rarely profitable, providing a working-class wage to a few people, including the owner. Today, however, one of the fastest growing and most profitable new ventures is a chain of barbershops in which each unit is run by a manager earning a middle-class salary. The two young owners applied management techniques, including a market survey and a three month training program for their managers.

The new entrepreneurs, says Drucker, tend to have management training, and they attend management seminars and programs in large numbers. Many become entrepreneurs only after they develop managerial experience in large organizations. Increasingly, management students at prestigious business schools see entrepreneurship as their ultimate goal.

Drucker also sees fundamental change going on in society. "Without doubt, the emergence of the entrepreneurial economy is as much a cultural and psychological event as it is an economic or technologcial one." His view is that the only thing government can effectively do is to remove obstacles to entrepreneurial growth. Drucker proposes exempting new enterprises for five to seven years from taxes on profits retained in the business.

Perhaps the high priest of futurologists is John Naisbitt, author of best-selling Megatrends. One of the megatrends he describes is the shift taking place from a managerial to an entrepreneurial society featuring the baby boomers. When they came of age in the 1970s and hit the job market, the economy was not at all in good shape. As a result, some of the baby boomers were forced into self-employment, and even entrepreneurship, by a weak job market. Others who valued their independence in the 1960s but had given it up for high paying jobs in corporations, were saving and plotting their escape into entrepreneurship. Naisbitt sees this as a continuing trend that will last into the next century.

Naisbitt, who lives in Washington, D.C., has gained a reputation as something of a champion of the Sun Belt. In May 1985, he was invited to address a conference of ten Sun Belt mayors in Austin, Texas. Speaking to an audience generally receptive to his message, Naisbitt served up several predictions regarding megatrends in society. Among them:

● The United States is headed for terrific labor shortages. Job seekers between now and the year 2000 will be searching in a seller's market.

● The "baby bust" generation is about to come of age. The number of teen-agers living in this country will decline by six million between 1980 and 1990. This is bad news for the likes of MacDonald's, where so many youth now find employment.

● Last year 700,000 new companies were started. In the relatively prosperous 1950s no more than 100,000 new firms were created in a single year. The entrepreneur has become America's "secret weapon, its engine of growth."

● The union movement and the welfare state are dead, both by-products of the late, unlamented industrial era.

● Travel and tourism will be big, as will retailing, in the coming years.

It is interesting to note that virtually all of the Sun Belt cities represented at the conference are into "pleasure" as a major element of their economies. They host millions of tourists a year and have large sports arenas that account for a substantial portion of the municipal economy. The mayors spent nearly an hour exchanging tales of the foreign trade missions they had taken in search of markets for their entrepreneurs' products, and in search of capital for their expansion.

The Small Business Sector

The definition of small business varies widely, depending upon the context. In the United States, a semi-legal definition is provided in the Small Business Act of 1953 which established the Small Business Administration. It states that a small business must be independently owned and operated and not dominant in its field of operation. The same Act provides the philosophical justification for small business (Sec. 2a):

> The essence of the American economic system of private enterprise is free competition. Only through full and free competition can free markets, free entry into business, and opportunities for the expression and growth of personal initiative and individual judgment be assured.

The question of size is addressed in the Act by attempting to match the numerical restrictions with the qualitative characteristics of each industry. In some industries it considers an enterprise with up to 1500 employees a small business, while in others 250 is the maximum. According to the Selective Service Act of 1948, a small business is one that employs fewer than 500 persons.

In her comparative study of the definitions of small business, Leah Hertz sums up the meaning of small business in the United States in the following manner:

● A small business does not necessarily have to be owned by a private individual, because the condition of "independent ownership" is interpreted widely to include majority shareholders and public quoted companies.

● The management of the small business need not be exclusive to its owner because the requirement for "independent operation" concerns "control" in a wider sense than the day-to-day management duties. And as the "control" stems from the ownership's rights, the actual management duties could be undertaken by hired managers who do not have ultimate control of the business.

● A small business does not have to be small in absolute terms, but only in relation to other enterprises within the same field of operation. Consequently, what is considered by the Small Business Act to be a small business might in real terms be a big one.

What constitutes the small business sector in the American economy? Dun and Bradstreet figures for 1984 indicate that by far the largest number of businesses with annual sales of less than $1 million are classified as eating establishments, which total nearly 175,000. In second place are gasoline service stations (100,000), drinking establishments and grocery stores (both 95,000). The fastest growing categories of business during the period from 1979 to 1984 are management/public relations (181 percent growth rate), beauty shops (153 percent), engineering and architectural services (110 percent). Those with a negative growth rate include hardware stores (-3.4 percent) furniture stores (-3.0 percent), auto equipment (-2.2 percent), women's ready-to-wear (-1.5), and gasoline stations (-0.3 percent).

Of the 11 million businesses in the United States, 10.8 million are categorized as small, with fewer than 500 employees. They employ about 50 million people, or half the nation's work force. They have generated more than half of the new product and service innovations developed in the last three decades.

Each year the President of the United States presents a report on The State of Small Business to the Congress. It is compiled by the Office of Advocacy of the Small Business Administration. The annual report issued in May 1985 announced that the key word for the U.S. economy and for small business in 1984 was growth. It noted that the dynamic small business sector showed an extraordinary capacity to mobilize resources and generate new growth in a changing economy. Small business-dominated industries added jobs at a rate almost twice that of industries dominated by large firms: 11.4 percent compared to only 5.3 percent from November 1982 through October 1984.

Two small business-dominated industries - retail trade and residential construction - continued the strong growth begun in 1983. Growth in the service industries, another sector with a major small business presence, also continued to be fueled by the demand for new products. For example, computer and data processing firms, advertising and mailing firms, and hotels registered sharply rising sales curves. Radio and television stores expanded sales by more than 20 percent, bakeries by 14 percent.

In the first half of 1984, entrepreneurs incorporated approximately 325,000 new businesses, an increase of 8.6 percent. Small business failure and bankruptcy rates remained fairly constant. Bankruptcy rates were down and failures were up less than one percent for the first six months of 1984 compared to the same period in 1983. Because of unfavorable business conditions in 1981 and 1982, fewer small firms had the resources available to stay in business until the latter half of 1983. Therefore, bankruptcy rates were higher in the first half of 1983 and lower in the second half.

Small business continued its traditional role as the major job generator in the American economy. A total of 5,676,000 new jobs were created from November 1982, at the bottom of the recession, through October 1984. A broader measure of employment change in the economy includes self-employment as well as wage and salary employment. This puts the total employment expansion for the period at 6,513,000, for an increase of 7.3 percent. Employment gains in small business-dominated industries in real estate, construction, finance, insurance, and services were impressive when compared with similar, large business-dominated industries. Fast-growing small business-dominated industries registered higher rates of employment growth than fast-growing large business-dominated industries. Relatively more establishments owned by the smallest enterprises with fewer than 20 employees showed constant employment, and relatively fewer show contracting employment. Establishments owned by the largest enterprises (more than 500 employees) appeared to exhibit declining employment.

The phenomenon of small business, while lacking in definition in nearly all countries, is being recognized for its role in job creation and innovation in Europe as well as the United States. European nations are faced with the highest levels of unemployment since World War II. They have increasingly rallied around the notion of local initiatives in general and in particular around small business development as a strategy for creating jobs. In the United States, the number of enterprises of 500 or fewer employees account for over 99 percent of the businesses, compared to an average of 90 percent in the European Common Market (EEC) countries. Employment in European small enterprises ranges from a low of 40 percent of the private sector work force in France to a high of 98 percent in Denmark, compared with 48 percent in the United States. Thus, on both sides of the Atlantic, small businesses play a major role as a percentage of total number of businesses, and as a percentage of private sector workforce.

High rates of unemployment and flat growth rates continue to plague Western Europe. As of April 1984, the EEC combined unemployment stood at over 10 percent. Formerly healthy economies such as the Netherlands and West Germany, where full employment was an implicit assumption, were crippled by 14.6 percent and 8.4 percent unemployment rates respectively. The EEC countries declared 1983 the Year of the Small and Medium Sized Enterprises. This initiative was taken for several reasons: There was a basic shift going on from a manufacturing to a service economy. Large manufacturing firms were facing hard times, many of them undergoing major worker displacement. And, the Europeans began taking note of the U.S. data on job creation in the small business sector.

David Birch points out that a large portion of European small businesses are what he calls income-substitution, low growth, businesses. A major difference in social-political disposition exists between the United States and Europe, according to Birch. It has to do with fear of failure. The American society is very forgiving of failure, whereas European societies tend to place tremendous value on stability and security. A great price is exacted for failure. In the United States you can declare bankruptcy, wipe out your debts, and start all over. In Europe, if you go bankrupt, everything you have - your personal reputation, your assets - everything goes with it. You are unlikely to ever get a loan again.

The American Entrepreneur

If European societies are characterized by constraints to individual entrepreneurial effort, small business in the United States has been a traditional path to independence for immigrants. Small business has provided a practical expression for the ideal of independence. The same entrepreneurial spirit that worked for Italian, Irish, and Jewish immigrants at the turn of the century is at work today for the Vietnamese, Koreans, Cubans, and other new Americans.

The "entrepreneurial mystique' was the focus of a special report on small business in The Wall Street Journal (May 1985). The report surveyed the results of a Gallup poll of a cross section of small businessmen running companies with sales of less than $50 million and 20 or more employees. This sample was compared with another group labeled "entrepreneurs", chief executives of companies listed by Inc. magazine as among the 500 fastest growing smaller companies in the country. Most of the companies in this category had more than doubled annual sales in the past five years. A third group consisted of Fortune 500 executives.

The respondents were almost exclusively male. The entrepreneurs - most of them under the age of 44 - were a generation younger than the corporate executives. While most entrepreneurs ran companies founded in the last ten years, the small business sample consisted of more established firms. The entrepreneurs were characterized as mavericks and dreamers, loners whose urge to do it their own way was in sharp contrast to the Fortune 500 executives. They were less distinguished students, more likely to have been expelled from school, less likely to have been student leaders or members of fraternities. All three groups showed an early inclination toward hard work, but the entrepreneurs exhibited a restlessness and rebelliousness not found among the corporate executives or the more traditional small business-owners. They also revealed a strong and early need to take charge. They were nearly twice as likely as the other executives to have operated a business while still in school.

The entrepreneurs were more ethnically diverse: 41 percent were from non Anglo-Saxon nationality groups, compared with only 15 percent of the corporate group and 17 percent of the small business group. Although most of the respondents came from middle class backgrounds, the successful entrepreneurs talked of childhoods characterized by hardship and economic constraints. They told of struggles to obtain financing, of 16-hour days and sleepless nights, of makeshift offices in garages and chicken hatcheries. And the willingness to take business risks.

The special report also profiled some of the more spectacular successes among the new immigrant groups and described how the old country network helps the newcomer to navigate the small business maze. The Korean community in Los Angeles is a case in point. One young Korean came to the United States in 1969 intending to be a teacher. But even with a master's degree in educatin, he couldn't find a job. He began selling auto parts to Korean-owned gas stations from the trunk of his car. Working day and night, he built an auto parts business. In 1974 he bought an old run-down store and eventually invested in a warehouse with a Korean immigrant partner. Sales gradually grew to over $500,000 a year. By the mid-1980s the area had become a thriving center of Korean small businesses, the largest concentration of Koreans in the country. Sociologists have noted that the Koreans have become America's new "middlemen minority" - those who act as traders and buffers between subordinated groups and the dominant society.

The question as to the nature of the American entrepreneur also guided Paul Dickson during two years of research in which he interviewed 200 self-employed businesspeople. They ranged across a wide spectrum of entrepreneurial interests, from one-person cottage industries, to mom and pop operations, to thriving firms with several employees. The common element was that they were independent risk-takers. Dickson dubbed his survey "Project Watercooler" since he was attempting to gather the kind of information people swap around water coolers in the office.

Dickson's survey results revealed a deep disregard for large institutions. The majority of his participants had left large organizations for various reasons. Some had devoted themselves to a coporation only to be out on the street because of lay-offs or managerial belt-tightening. These are the ones who vowed "never again." In addition to the disillusionment with corporate life, the respondents shared the desire to get out from under the boss's thumb and become their own boss. They tended to cite discipline and determination as the personal characteristics more useful in establishing an independent career. Self confidence and willingness to take risks ranked next, followed by the ability to communicate with others in conversation as well as in writing. Persistence ranked high as well, including the ability to work through illnesses and long hours. The entrepreneurs worked an average of 50 hours a week, some putting in up to 60 hours while others prided themselves on being able to manage with 38 to 42 hours a week.

Dickson's entrepreneurs cited the ability to serve others and provide a good product as among the most important rewards for their efforts. Another reward mentioned was the ability to find work and get paid for it without going through a lot of middlemen. Success and recognition were of course also cited as rewards. Freedom, control, and independence were also consistently mentioned as significant rewards. Oddly enough, the entrepreneurs did not mention that computers and technological advances were a factor in attracting them to independence, even those in the software business. The respondents from electronic cottages noted that it was not the electronics that appealed to them, but that the technology made it easier. But a majority of the participants said that they were planning to add a computer to the tools of their trade.

Dickson asked his entrepreneurs to suggest some of the lessons learned from their experience. The following were among the most frequently mentioned lessons:

● Make sure you choose a field that you really love. You have to decide whether you just want to make money or want to "make a living."

● Ignore all the negative statistics which tell you that 95 percent of all new businesses fail in the first eight years. Dwelling on such data is like staying up on your wedding night to study the divorce statistics.

● Don't be too cautious about starting your business. You won't be executed for going bankrupt.

● Have a clear idea of your goals. Review your goals periodically and don't make all of them long-term.

● Don't base a new business on a single client or customer. If you have to rely on key clients, have as many as possible. A business should be able to survive the loss of its best customer.

● If you are married, make sure your spouse understands what you are up to, including all the inherent risks, especially if joint savings are on the line.

● Don't expect a new business to be an overnight success.

Intraprenurship

The entreprenurial revolution among small businesses has forced large corporations to devise ways of responding to the movement. While many employees of large corporations are jumping ship in order to be on their own because they feel stifled by the corporate environment, others are staying on and looking for ways to innovate within the company. This phenomenon has come to be known as "intrapreneurship" - intra-company entrepreneurship. Gifford Pinchot III, a New Haven management consultant whose clients include many large corporations, has coined this term to describe what he sees happening in the corporate world. His book on intrapreneuring is based on research among 20 major companies that have sought ways to stimulate innovation.

Pinchot observes that too often the corporation becomes a maze of feudal empires, suspicious of each other. People on the way up see the competition, not out there in the marketplace, but internally in the form of other individuals competing for the top jobs. The intrapreneurial efforts he now sees going on within corporations were of course underway long before he named the process. He has helped focus attention on this challenge of finding a way of managing in a more decentralized manner.

One such effort is taking place at Xerox Square in Rochester, New York, where a team of 15 intrapreneurs is at work designing new products for the company. The unit was created in 1971 as a troubleshooting organization. By the end of the 1970s the team had evolved into a "concept house" working outside of the company's product development organization. By identifying the "voids in the product line" the intrapreneurs came up with the idea for the Xerox 2600 copier, which became a highly profitable product innovation.

Pinchot observes that although large corporations have the ability to manage inventors, they are incapable of managing the entrepreneurial function. The way to manage innovation is to choose the right people and give them freedom. With his desire to turn vision into reality, the intrapreneur usually does not trust people in other departments to support his or her projects. The first stumbling block for the innovator in a large corporation is marketing. Traditionally, the person who initiates the project lacks objectivity about its future stages and is seldom involved in marketing research. This is bad innovation policy. The intrapreneur needs to communicate with outside people and customers.

At the same time, intrapreneurs can enjoy tremendous advantages inside large corporations. They have access to the marketing channels and production facilities of the organization. There are both financial and human resources available that can be tapped without concern over confidentiality. When the corporation recognizes the advantages it can offer the innovator, an environment can be created in which it is easier to innovate inside than it is outside the company.

Obstacles to Small Business

The entrepreneurial economy has its downside as well. From 1979 to 1980, bankruptcy filings by large and small businesses in the United States increased 56 percent, from 29,500 to 46,050. The figure rose to over 66,000 in 1981. The bulk of business bankruptcies around the country involve very small enterprises, many of them unincorporated. This allows their proprietors, often one or two people, to receive the same kinds of exemptions usually restricted to personal bankruptcies under Chapter 7 of the Bankruptcy Reform Act of 1978. Though business bankruptcies have been increasing since 1979, they are actually a small part of the cases of business failure. For every one bankruptcy, there are 10 or 15 other business terminations in which people pay off their bills, close their doors, and simply stop doing business.

Many bankruptcies in the Washington, D.C., area in the early 1980s were related to downturns in the construction industry. Others, particularly Washington-based consultant groups and associations, were related to a reduction in government spending. On the other hand, fewer new businesses were being started. Because people were able to get risk-free earnings by investing in Treasury securities, they were unwilling to risk starting up a new business. Nearly 60 percent of new businesses in the United States begin with personal savings as their major source of capital. Such businesses automatically start off as high-risk ventures. In effect, the government was competing against the small businessperson.

Many small businesses have difficulty obtaining credit from banks for their operations. While big companies borrow well below the prime rate, small firms have to settle for two or three percentage points above the prime if they can even get a loan. Banks are themselves in business to make a profit. They will frequently tell a small business loan applicant to go to another bank because they cannot make enough money on a $25,000 loan.

During the early 1980s, many small businesses found relationships with banks increasingly uncomfortable. The banks began to raise the fees they charged for their services far beyond the general rise of prices. Some banks even began turning their backs on small business customers of many years. Many small banks, themselves small businesses, were being gobbled up by bigger banks because their costs were running far ahead of their small-town fees. They could no longer remain insulated from economic trends beyond their local community. For their part, the banks contended that dealing with small business was more time consuming, costlier, and more risky than dealing with larger companies.

Bankers point out that it often takes a lot more time and effort to determine the creditworthiness of a small business than of a major corporation. More paperwork is involved, especially if the loan is guaranteed by the Small Business Administration. The income earned on a small business loan, even at a high rate is small compared with that earned on a big loan. Banks have often increased their fees to cover the cost of services. However, a small business that manages to maintain a high enough balance in its checking account may escape paying direct fees.

A major problem in the relationships between small businesses and their bankers is that the entrepreneurs do not fit easily into the corporate modes established by the banks. From the banker's perspective, a business is expected to maintain records similar to those of large firms, a practice that many smaller firms find too time consuming. The small business person looks for a personal relationship in which the banker understands the basic problems of his or her business.

Some banks, in trying to build their small business division, seem to be doing just the opposite of what the small businesses say they need. For example, Chase Manhattan set up a special unit to deal with loan applications from small firms. The applications are gathered at branches and sent to the special unit. But in moving the loan approval process beyond the branches, it also separates the function from the business person. Some banks that have geared up efficiently for small business loans have become enthusiastic about the field, however. In some cases, these loans can actually be more lucrative than lending to bigger companies with more bargaining power.

In his survey of entrepreneurs, Paul Dickson identified several common problems faced by small businesses:

● Self-employment tax. You must pay the employee's and the employer's share of Social Security. By 1990, a self-employed person will have to pay twice as much as his or her employed counterpart.

● Health and disability insurance. More small businesses encounter difficulty in obtaining coverage. A disabled veteran

38

complained that he could not buy health insurance, although he was eventually able to get it as part of his wife's plan.

● Licensing. This can amount to a Catch 22. One man noted that his state licensing requirements almost demand that you be in business or doing the business you are trying to be licensed for before you are accepted for the licensing examination.

● Personal credit and bank loans. Many of Dickson's respondents complained that they could get credit cards when they had a "regular" job, but they were having trouble getting them as self employed persons.

● Bans on working at home - federal, state, and local. A typical response was that running a business out of your home was illegal in the local area. Some get around the problem by using a post office box and not notifying the local government.

The Political Agenda of Small Business

Is small business simply another entry in the dreary list of special interest groups that see Uncle Sam as a source of almost unlimited largesse? Or does small business have a more expansive political identity that describes an essential and dynamic sector of the national economy with an overriding stake in major economic issues? These questions provide the framework in which to examine the small business political agenda in the United States. Some proponents of small business contend that the time is ripe to fundamentally refashion the tax system and redefine fiscal policy. They believe that it is time to move beyond competing for a small business share of the federal dole and on to issues that are at the top of the nation's agenda.

For its part, the Reagan administration sought to embrace the entrepreneurial movement while treating the small business lobby as just another special interest group. As President Reagan was extolling the virtues of entrepreneurship and declaring the Age of the Entrepreneur at hand, his budget cutters were sharpening their knives with an eye toward abolishing federal programs of assistance to small businesses. The mantle of hero of small business seemed ill-fitted for a President whose political career was closely intertwined with big business interests. But then, the mantle did not appear to be tailored for any one politician as Americans began to chart public policies in the second half of the 1980s.

● The Small Business Administration: A Litmus Test

The Small Business Administration (SBA), created by Congress in 1953, is but one of hundreds of federal agencies in Washington. Like other agencies, the SBA has its proponents and adversaries. In early 1985, the SBA bobbed like a cork atop a menacing wave of opposition from the Reagan administration. David Stockman, director of the Office of Management and Budget, was intent on eliminating the SBA, along with other federal lending programs. In testimony before the Senate Small Business Committee he argued that in an era of $200 billion deficits the SBA was one luxury the government could no longer afford. Stockman claimed that the agency, with a current annual budget of $730 million, "indiscriminately sprays a faint mist of subsidized credit into the weakest and most prosaic nooks and crannies" of the economy. He noted that the SBA serves only a tiny minority - less than 0.2 percent of the nation's small businesses. Even worse, he said, 60 percent of the SBA's help goes to firms in the wholesale, retail, and service sectors where he claimed there were already too many small businesses.

The administration proposed to close down the "rathole" (Stockman's term) for good, and to discontinue all its loan programs. The loan portfolio at the time amounted to $9.8 billion worth at face value. It then would be turned over to the Treasury, which would sell it off at a fraction of par. The agency's other functions, consisting primarily of advice to fledgling businesses, would be transferred to the Commerce Department. Stockman estimated the total savings of the proposed manoeuvre at $5.3 billion.

However, there were both political and economic factors which conspired to keep the SBA afloat. Not the least of the political factors was the fact that the agency enjoys considerable support in Congress. A disproportionate number of SBA loans go to small businesses in the district of members of Congress and the Senate who happen to sit on the Small Business Committees. Economic factors provide a rather more equitable justification for continuing SBA programs. Friends of the agency pointed out that wiping out federal economic development and small business lending would be penny wise and pound foolish. After the storm of administration criticism and a spate of negative media attention, however, the SBA floated back to the surface, battered but not beaten.

It is worth examining the issues involved because they help set the framework for long term policy considerations affecting small business. While granting some of the political arguments against the SBA, the economic justification for its programs is persuasive. Friends of the SBA pointed out that programs which

40

aid small business growth and expansion cost taxpayers nothing because the new payroll, business and property taxes they generate far exceed program costs.

In the past ten years four federal programs, including the SBA's 503 Certified Development Company (CDC) and the Small Business Investment Company (SBIC), have created over 1 million jobs nationwide. They have pumped billions of dollars into the U.S. Treasury. For example, the SBIC has provided over $2 billion in equity capital to 70,000 entrepreneurs and created 250,000 jobs since 1958. An independent cost benefit analysis found that for fiscal 1979 there was a direct return to the Treasury of $110 for each dollar spent on the SBIC. In the final analysis, then, federal small business loan programs actually help reduce the budget deficits by generating revenues.

It is true that SBA programs reach only a tiny portion of small businesses. Many of them have needs that are unmet by existing institutions. The growth of small businesses often is stunted by their inability to obtain long-term capital. Large corporations, by contrast, have little trouble getting 20-year loans at fixed rates from insurance companies or on Wall Street in order to finance new plants and equipment. Such is not the case for small businesses who must rely on local banks that are regulated short-term lenders – three to five years at best. Hence, small and medium sized companies are faced with a serious problem in the long-term credit market when it comes time to expand.

Public sector partnerships such as the SBA program help in a modest way to fill those needs. They encourage private investors to make the capital investments that they would not otherwise make without a private-public joint venture. Up to 40 percent of long-term lending to small businesses have an SBA guarantee, which encourages banks to make loans with longer terms and at fixed rates. Sometimes the SBA's loan guarantee program has been the small firm's answer to long-term financing needs. But for each small business that is assisted in this manner, there are hundreds of others who are not so fortunate. There is a wide array of notions about whether and how to stimulate the small business sector in the United States, each carrying public policy implications.

In January 1985, as the Reagan Administration's plan to abolish the Small Business Administration gathered strength in Washington, more than 100 small business activists met in Scottsdale, Arizona, to try to resolve the question of their political identity and to develop a strategy. It was the fourth annual leadership conference of Small Business United (SBU), an umbrella lobbying organization comprised of a dozen regional small business groups from around the country. The purpose of the meeting, similar in style to a political convention, was to adopt a narrow platform of legislative priorities for the first session of the 99th Congress.

Ambivalence about the Small Business Administration dominated the strategy debate. Tom Powers, general counsel of the House Small Business Committee, told the conference that they should all consider attempts to abolish the SBA a personal insult. Representatives from the Southwest tended to take a different view. They opposed what they considered special interest groups that insist on having their own agency in Washington. They urged the conference to make tax reform and deficit reduction its top priority for the future. A majority of the conference participants, however, held to the traditional view that the SBA was an important link to power in Washington.

The already limited political clout of small business in Washington was threatened by political schisms reflected at the Scottsdale meeting. The two top legislative priorities for 1985 identified in balloting among the conference participants were saving the Small Business Administration and reducing the federal deficit. Tax simplification came next. Some of the participants, such as the SBU's immediate past president Jack Rennie, decried the lack of long range planning and failure not to look beyond tactical or topical issues. The leadership vacuum within SBU and other small business lobbies described by Rennie could carry political costs. When small business advocates espouse a political vision that is narrowly parochial, they risk the loss of visibility and access in Washington.

Some voices are beginning to be raised in favor of attempting to reach a consensus on overall strategic objectives and developing an annual as well as a long-range plan to achieve them. This would give the entrepreneurial sector a coherent voice in national debates over tax, foreign trade, and economic policies, the kind of influence small business has never had. They argue against proposals that encourage smallness for its own sake or that reward inefficiency and dependency. They advocate educating policymakers to the fact that risk, entrepreneurship, innovation, and growth are not liberal or conservative issues. Rather they represent an urgent national priority which Congress must address if the United States is to maintain its competitiveness in world markets and create jobs.

● A Legislative Agenda for Small Business?

President Reagan has spoken of his goal of an America bursting with opportunity in an Age of the Entrepreneur. His plan for achieving this goal involves a tax program that would

42

lower personal tax rates, thus giving a boost to the nearly 15 million small businesses which are individual proprietorships. To further promote business formation, he proposed to reduce the maximum corporate tax rate from 46 to 33 percent. He claimed that since most small corporations would pay even lower rates, they could lead the way in creating jobs for all who wanted to work.

The Reagan administration plan for small business may be summed up in a word: tax incentives. For several years the administration has promoted a controversial program that would use tax incentives. The relaxation of certain standards and regulations would encourage small businesses to locate in the designated zones. The administration cites the experience in Great Britain, where the concept of enterprise zones was born, to illustrate that blighted areas can be turned into productive neighborhoods.

This is a rather old idea which Congress has rejected on several occasions. Critics of the plan are concerned that the incentives being offered would simply lead established businesses to relocate into the zones rather than fostering new business start-ups. According to polls conducted by the National Federation of Independent Business (NFIB), small business owners opposed the concept of federal enterprise zones by a two to one margin on two separte occasions. An NFIB study of the problems of small business owners in 85 cities suggested that the problems of starting a business do not focus on tax incentives. Most small business people just getting started do not make enough money to pay much income tax on their earnings. Rather, their problems center on the need for access to capital, availability of skilled labor, and affordable insurance

The State of Small Business report depicts the recent expansion in the small business sector as being part of the overall economic growth experienced in normal patterns of a recovery. It suggests that the economy as a whole and small business in particular have benefited from the deregulation of specific industries. The report's supply-side economic orientation is premised on the assumption that private markets act perfectly when the role of government is minimized. It argues vehemently against proposals for a national industrial policy, based on the premise that small businesses are already responding to the long-term structural changes in the economy. It maintains that through entrepreneurship, expansion, and innovations, small businesses are redistributing resources within and among industries through existing market mechanisms. Policies should instead create an economic environment that does not inhibit the growth of small businesses, which are providing the impetus for industrial change.

There are those who do not share the administration's attitude of benign neglect toward small business. Some of them, in fact, entertain presidential aspirations. Perhaps it is premature to argue, only weeks after an inauguration, that presidential politics is already in the making. But Joel Kotkin, writing for Inc. magazine in November 1984, predicted that small business would be the issue of 1988. Kotkin described a growing number of young politicians from both political parties who are casting their lot with small business. "What makes them different," he said, "is that they see entrepreneurs not just as a special interest group or a collection of special interest groups, but as the heart of a new American political economy."

Kotkin illustrated the political dimension of the entrepreneurial economy with examples from both the Republican and Democratic parties. Reps. Ed Zschau of California and Jack Kemp of New York, both Republicans, endorse a program emphasizing a minor government role and the maximum use of incentives to spur entrepreneurial growth. Kemp's "opportunity society" represents a conscious shift away from the country club norms of traditional Republican politics. By creating enterprise zones to spur business activities in ghetto areas, Kemp hopes to turn inner-city residents into owners of small businesses.

On the Democratic side, Rep. Charles Schumer of New York represents a growing congressional conviction that small business is crucial to the party's survival. He differs radically from the so called Atari Democrats, who talk of targeting the high-tech sector of the economy. In May 1984, Schumer introduced a bill to the House Committee on Banking, Finance and Urban Affairs known as the National Entrepreneurship Act, designed to help ensure that existing financial institutions are better equipped to provide adequate financing on affordable terms for new entrepreneurial ventures. It would set up a secondary market for industrial mortgages, spur investments in small firms by loosening regulations on pension funds, and encourage bank loans to new firms by establishing a special loan loss reserve fund.

The National Entreprneurship Act has the following titles:

● Loan loss reserve fund. The fund would insure banks against losses and defaults on loans to new businesses. It would be financed by small payments from banks, borrowers, and the federal government.

● Matching grants for state venture capital/royalty finance corporations. Royalty finance is a form of long term "patient" capital that provides for an investor's return to be based on a percentage of the sale revenues generated by each new product. It would allow new business to undertake longer term projects because it would not have to start paying investors until the product or innovation is a commercial success.

- Pension investment units. Public and private pension funds have more than $850 billion in assets. However, state and federal laws often prevent pension fund managers from investing these assets in the securities of new businesses. The federal government would make available matching grants to encourage the establishment of state sponsored pension investment units. Their purpose would be to recommend changes in state pension fund regulations and provide research about the investment opportunities of new entrepreneurial businesses in their states.

- Secondary market for industrial mortgages. Commerical banks specialize in short term business lending and have the facilities to evaluate loan applications and service the large number of small loans needed by new businesses. Pension funds and insurance companies are a major source of long term capital, but they are not well equipped to service large numbers of small business loans. A government sponsored secondary mortgage market would purchase industrial mortgages from banks and resell them to pension funds and insurance companies.

Democrats like Schumer who are eager to be identified as populists make the point that the real enemy of small business is big business because it gets all the breaks a small business can never get. Schumer argues that corporate income tax subsidizes the borrowing costs of profitable, already established companies. In effect, this penalizes entrepreneurs during the unprofitable start-up period, who must pay higher after tax interest rates. Federal banking regulations tell entrepreneurs that they cannot qualify for a loan unless they have collateral, giving rise to the observation that bankers will lend entrepreneurs money only if they can first prove that they don't need it!

On the Senate side, the National Entrepreneurship Act was introduced by Sen. Gary Hart (D./Colorado) in the first session of the 99th Congress in April 1985. It was one of three bills which Hart sponsored to provide education and training in a changing economy. In remarks entered into the Congressional Record, Hart maintained that by making risk and long-term capital available to new and small businesses, the provisions of the legislation would unleash America's entrepreneurial energies. Hart pointed out that during the recession years of 1981 and 1982, small firms created 2.8 million new jobs, more than off-setting the nearly 1.7 million jobs lost in the large industrial sector. He added that the jobs created by these firms were par-ticularly crucial because of opportunities provided for min-orities and women. Finally, he said, small enterprises produce four times as many innovations per research and development

45

dollar as medium sized firms, and 24 times as many as large businesses.

It could well be, however, that the most substantive political change in favor of small business in coming years will be at the state rather than the national level. County and state governments are already enacting and implementing programs to invest in new entreprise development. These efforts recognize the importance of new and small businesses in generating jobs, new products, and economic opportunity. Unfortunately, many state efforts are flawed by some of the same problems that have plagued more traditional programs. Scarce public funds are being misspent by providing opportunities to firms already well established. Often the types of assistance offered are inappropriate.

Most state enterprise development programs are focusing on the capital problems of small and new businesses. The real problem is both the amount and type of capital available, not the cost. The private capital market often operates in a way that prevents well-managed firms from obtaining needed financing. Capital markets can "fail" for various reasons. A market failure occurs, for example, whenever capital is not allocated to ventures on the basis of their expected rate of return. And capital markets may not operate equitably. The way in which money is allocated may violate people's sense of justice. There are numerous reasons why private capital markets may not function effectively. Suppliers of capital may be prejudiced against some ventures for racial, sexual, or political reasons. Investors may not have accurate information about new and small firms.

States must seek to encourage the huge private capital sources - both institutions and individuals - in order to allocate more funds to new enterprises. One of the vehicles being used to obtain this objective is the establishment of incubators. These are facilities that support the early stage development of new ventures through the provision of such services as low rent, flexible leases, support services, and management advice - thereby serving as a "hatchery" for new businesses and new jobs. One of the advantages of the incubator approach is that the "hatched" firms are more apt to stay in the area and provide a source of long-term job opportunities. Local entrepreneurs are more likely to have an atachment to the area than are decision-makers in a larger corporate branch plant.

By the time President Reagan made his pronouncement about the Age of the Entrepreneur to a Wall Street group in the spring of 1985, it had already been a buzzword for several years. It was still too early to tell whether the entrepreneurial revival was mainly a function of technology, of the digital computer, or whether it went beyond to a basic restructuring of society. In political terms, it was certainly unclear whether the movement would reach such proportions as to propel a savvy politician to the White House, as some have suggested possible. Certainly few were talking about the implications of a small business agenda on a global scale. The following chapters examine the small business sector in the Third World, as well as the policies that have only begun to attempt to stimulate it.

Chapter Two References

Alvin Toffler, Previews and Promises, New York: Bantam Books, 1983.

Paul Dickson, "The New Entrepreneurs: The Urge Intensifies," Creative Living (Winter 1985), pp. 2-7.

Paul Taylor, "Forecast Calls for Fun in the Sun Belt," Washington Post, May 25, 1985.

David Birch, interviewed by INC. magazine, April 1985.

INC. magazine, June 1985, scorecard on small business in the U.S. from Dun & Bradstreet.

Renee A. Berger, "The Small Business Incubator: Lessons Learned from Europe," prepared under contract with the Office of Private Sector Initiatives, Small Business Administration, Washington, D.C. (no date).

Warren Brown, "Debt Burden Forcing More Area Firms to Bankruptcy," Washington Post, May 24, 1982.

Robert Bennett, "How Banks are Squeezing Small Business," New York Times," April 25, 1982.

Robert Tucker, "Intrapreneuring - Creating the Entrepreneurial Spirit within the Corporation," Creative Living (Winter 1985), pp. 27-32.

"A Special Report: Small Business", The Wall Street Journal, May 20, 1985.

Steve Coll, "Beyond Uncle Sam and His Gifts," in INC. magazine, May 1985, pp. 22-24.

The State of Small Business: A Report of the President, transmitted to the Congress, May 1985, Washington, D.C. Smal Business Administration.

Sara Loveland, "Saving Federal Small Business and Economic Development Programs," The Entrepreneurial Economy, Monthly Review of Enterprise Development Strategies, Washington, D.C.: Corporation for Enterprise Development, April 1985 (Volume 4, No. 10).

John Sloan, "Federal Enterprise Zones Miss the Mark," The Entrepreneurial Economy, April 1985.

Chapter Three

Small Business in the Third World

"The national bourgeoisie of underdeveloped countries must not be opposed only because it threatens to slow down the total harmon-ious development of the nation.   It must simply be stoutly op-posed because, literally, it is good for nothing."

> – Franz Fanon
> The Wretched of the Earth, 1968

"Where in our lands are those citizens who have sufficient capital to establish modern industries?   And second, how would our infant industries fight other capitalist enterprises?   As a general rule, no individual, or group of individuals from within our nations has the capacity to establish even a large modern textile mill, or run a large scale commercial enterprise.   That amount of money, and that kind of expertise just do not exist."

> – Julius Nyerere
> Freedom and Development, 1973

"...Les problèmes auxquels se heurtent les petites et moyennes entreprises (PME) sont nombreux et divers; on parle surtout des problèmes financiers dus à l'insuffisance des fonds propres et des fonds de roulement...Pour qu'une PME puisse survivre, il est indispensable que l'environnement lui soit favorable...et que soit lancée une politique économique stimulante pour les PME."

"...The problems which small and medium-sized enterprises face are numerous and diverse.   Above all, there are the financial problems owing to insufficient funds. In order for a small/medium sized enterprise to survive, it is indispensible that the envi-ronment be favorable, and that a stimulating economic policy be established."

> – Alexandre Keipo, Editor
> Le Manager (Abidjan), August 1983

49

The Third World is a term that is used to mean those developing countries which belong neither to the capitalist Western bloc nor to the communist Eastern bloc. There is some disagreement as to whether this includes the People's Republic of China and other developing countries such as Vietnam. Some argue that the latter nations belong to the Second World because they have apparently opted out of the capitalist system. It is not our purpose here to debate the fine distinctions in terminology. There is, however, evidence to suggest that China has moved in recent years toward a reinterpretation of Marxist ideology to incorporate profit motives in an attempt to stimulate small scale enterprises at the local level.

There is even less agreement as to what constitutes small enterprise in the developing world. There is no universally acknowledged definition of its size or role in economic development. The economies of most developing countries are characterized by a combination of large state-owned enterprises and those owned by foreign investors on the one hand, and a wide range of small and micro-enterprises operating in the informal sector on the other. Often policy statements of governments in developing countries tend to consist of generalities embracing the small and medium-scale enterprise sector without providing measures to resolve the considerable problems which they face. Indeed, the actions of national governments combined with the behavior of private sector investors and speculators often lead to the suppression of small enterprises.

An illustration of the extent to which Third World economies are dominated by state-owned enterprises (often called parastatals) and foreign investors is to be found in a special issue of Jeune Afrique Economique (December 1984). The third annual survey of the 700 leading industrial firms in 18 francophone African countries is modeled after the U.S. Fortune 500. The African continent - francophone countries in particular - may provide an extreme case in point, compared with other regions of the Third World. The survey arrives at several general conclusions. The majority of the enterprises in these countries are those in which the state is the principal owner, although there is an "air of privatization" in a few of the countries surveyed, such as Tunisia and Morocco. Many of the largest ones are owned predominantly by foreign investors. While their growth in earnings compares favorably with companies in the industrialized countries, many of these firms register modest and sometimes negative profit rates. In any case, there is no automatic correlation between poor profit rates and state ownership; privately owned companies also have trouble showing a profit.

The Jeune Afrique Ecnomique survey reveals some interesting patterns. For example, there is only one company within the
top ten in Cameroun that is owned by private nationals. Among
the top five, one is 100 percent owned by foreign interests and
two others are over 65 percent owned by foreigners. A similar
situation obtains in the Ivory Coast, where one company in the
top ten is 100 percent owned by nationals. Three of the top ten
are fully owned by foreigners. In only three does the state have
a majority interest. In Zaire, three of the four largest enterprises are 100 percent state-owned, although in six of the top
ten foreigners hold a majority interest.

In contrast to this pattern, in Morocco six of the top ten
enterprises are predominantly owned by private nationals, three
of them 100 percent owned. In none of them do foreign interests
account for more than 50 percent. Indeed, the overwhelming
majority of the 147 Moroccan enterprises listed are owned by private nationals, and only a handful are state-owned. A rather
different pattern emerges in Tunisia, where eight of the top ten
companies are primarily state-owned. In none of the largest
enterprises are foreign interests predominant. However, only the
smaller companies among the 138 in Tunisia are owned by private
nationals. Finally, among the smaller countries such as Chad and
Niger there is scarcely any participation of private nationals in
the larger enterprises.

Atop the list of the 25 largest enterprises in the survey is
the petroleum company, Elf Gabon, which is 75 percent foreign
owned. The same is true for the second largest company in the
survey, Elf Congo. Only seven of the companies on the list are
wholly owned by the state, and only two are fully owned by
private nationals. Half of all the firms on the list are either
Moroccan or Tunisian. The typical arrangement is for the company
to be jointly owned by state and foreign interests.

Small Business and Theories of Development

As Ray Bromley pointed out in a recent anthology, the role
of small enterprise in development has been debated by scholars
for over a century. Anarchists and Marxists fell out over the
issue as early as 1872. There developed a schism between
advocates of small enterprises, participatory democracy, "appropriate technology", and decentralization on the one hand, and
advocates of rapid industrialization, "advanced technology", mass
production, and increasingly centralized government on the other.
Those who devised policies for the support of small- scale producers were tarred with Lenin's brush as "petite-bourgeoisie theo-
rists." They were accused of wishing to postpone industrialization and the workers' revolution.

Bromley suggests that however relevant these polemics remain to development studies, they can not possibly be considered to offer the definitive word on small enterprises. The world economy and political system have changed enormously over the past century, including technological advances affecting many forms of economic activity. The Anarchist dream of the gradual decomposition and overthrow of the State seems ever more remote. The Marxist dream of the global crisis of capitalism and the overthrow of bourgeois rule through proletarian revolution in the most advanced capitalist countries does not appear to be at hand.

However, there has been a remarkable persistence of small enterprises in the midst of diverse changes both at the world level and within developing countries. These enterprises have been created, transformed, and destroyed in a variety of contexts and are still in abundance in every corner of the globe. They co-exist with large state and private enterprises, often performing subordinate or complementary roles. Everywhere there are high birth and death rates for small enterprises, accompanied by notable capacities for adaptation and innovation. The relative importance of small enterprises in the economy may be higher in capitalist countries than in socialist countries. But even in the COMECON states of Eastern Europe, there are millions of legal cooperatives as well as illegal small enterprises, and little indication of a decline in their importance.

The slow pace of industrialization in most of the Third World and the global economic crisis of the 1970s and 1980s would appear to diminish the likelihood of the Marxist-Leninist scenario of proletarianization and a workers' revolution. Moreover, there is little evidence to support Lenin's claim that "large-scale machine industry completely squeezes out the small enterprises." Rather, small enterprises are in a continuous state of flux, characterized by new beginnings, expansions, contractions, and extinctions. They adjust to the expansion and contraction of larger industries and play a role in both the causes and effects of the changing structure of the economy.

At the same time, most of the liberal and neo-classical analyses of Third World economies have employed a dualistic approach as a theoretical basis. They posit two distinct sectors: the "modern" or "formal" sector on the one hand, and the "traditional", "backward", or "informal" sector on the other. In their simplest form, such divisions reflect a distinction between large, capitalist enterprises and government activities (modern formal), and small-scale workshops, cottage industries, and peasant enterprises (informal). The latter existed before, and continue in the face of, Western capitalist penetration. Modern industries are those which result directly from foreign influence and investment, the application of advanced technology

52

and sophisticated professional and government activities.

Critics of this approach such as Francisco de Oliveira have reviewed the informal sector concept from a different perspective. They have helped establish a trend towards studies of small enterprises within the context of the "total" economy rather than as some sort of autonomous small enterprise sector. de Oliveira, a Brazilian social scientist, has mounted a concerted attack on "crude dependency theories" which imply that there is no hope of sustained capitalist economic development in the Third World. He explains how and why petty production not only survives in co-existence with capitalist industrialization, but may actually increase in significance by performing roles which are essentially complementary to large-scale production. He further shows how new enterprises may be founded to perform functions which did not even exist before the advent of industrialization or large-scale imports of consumer goods.

The de Oliveira essay, written in 1972 and based on two decades of research on the Brazilian economy since 1930, examines its structural transformation and reconstitution of the conditions necessary for the expansion of the capitalist mode of production. It is theoretically entirely opposed to the dualist approach and breaks with the "underdevelopment" school of development studies. He argues that the Brazilian experience – and that of many other underdeveloped countries – shows that even with fully developed capitalist relations of production in the industrial sector, non-capitalist patterns of production are perpetuated in the agricultural sector.

The Role of the Entrepreneur in Development

There is a growing body of literature which seeks to describe and understand the role of the entrepreneur in the development process. Raymond Brown reviewed this literature in a doctoral dissertation in 1982. He observed that when economists first looked at Third World economic development issues they tended to superimpose classical models of development. Natural resources were perceived as the key to the process, then capital was considered to be the main ingredient. Recently the focus has tended to shift to innovations in technology and the need for "change-oriented" value systems. Other disciplines such as psychology, sociology, and anthropology have been used to explain the entrepreneurial process.

Max Weber's classical study of the Protestant ethic has been held up to non-Western societies in an attempt to explain development. It is generally recognized that Weber's work ethic is not confined to Protestants or to Christians for that matter! In each society there seem to be some groups with a greater propensity to become entrepreneurs than others: Quakers, Jews, Lebanese, Scotch Irish, Mormons, the Ibos of Nigeria, and the Antioquenos of Colombia to mention but a few. Entrepreneurs in Japan, Switzerland, and Israel have managed to develop their economies without the presence of abun-dant indigenous natural resources. Often displaced refugee and immigrant populations demonstrate an unusually high degree of entrepreneurial activity. Koreans immigrants in the United States today provide a notable example.

Another well known economist, E.E. Hagen, constructed a general thesis of economic development which explained entrepreneurship as the result of lower status groups seeking non-traditional avenues for self-realization through creative economic ventures. In his view, the values of traditional societies constrain the development process. Development, which he defined as essentially a technological process, depends upon creative individuals. Since authoritarian types are dominant in traditional societies, the emergence of entrepreneurs is inhibited. Hagen saw the critical factor leading to the breakdown of traditional bonds and the emergence of creative entrepreneurial activity as being "status respect withdrawal." This occurs when a group of people in society lose their status and are forced to find new sources of status recognition. Entrepreneurial activity is one alternative for attaining new status.

More recently, Albert Shapero has taken an entirely different approach, choosing as his unit of analysis the "entrepreneurial event," rather than the entrepreneur as an individual. His approach places less importance on economic factors and seeks to explain the event through social and political factors as well. Shapero attempts to avoid the question as to whether an individual who has carried out an entrepreneurial act is or is not an entrepreneur. He is concerned to consider the one-time entrepreneur as well as the full time entrepreneur. He believes that the entrepreneurial event is in itself an innovative act; there is no need to bind the event to the emergence of new productive technologies. His break with traditional approaches is in seeking to encompass initiatives and risk-taking behaviors in all sectors, not just economic. Shapero's model aims at explaining the one-time promoter, intrapreneurship within large corporations, and even activities within civic settings as well as in planned economies.

To approach this objective, Shapero drew upon data from studies done on unique events surrounding company formations in various countries, economic sectors, and time periods. He described the process of change in the "life path" of individuals that kept them from moving in a given direction. He submitted that the research indicates that individuals are more likely to

54

take action upon negative information rather than positive. Negative displacement precipitates more company formations than do positive possibilities. Shapero points out that historically, extreme externally imposed displacement of political and religious refugee groups is often associated with entrepreneurial events. Examples are numerous: North Africans who have settled in France, Lebanese and Pakistanis in West Africa, and Palestinians throughout the Middle East.

Students of Third World development have sought to ascertain whether there was something unique in the economic and social environment of developing countries which explains the problems of entrepreneurial development. In December 1981, there was an international colloquium on African enterprises and entrepreneurs held in Paris. It was organized under the auspices of the Agence de Cooperation Culturelle et Technique, created in 1970 and grouping francophone countries around the world. The participants addressed the question of the definition of African enterprise. Is it anything other than the result of the colonial experience and the introduction of Western capitalism? What, then, is the role of the informal sector, of indigenous enterprises which account for a sizeable proportion of production and capital? And what is the role of the African entrepreneur in the relations of domination and dependence that govern the international system?

An understanding of present day conditions was sought by examining the colonial era. In some instances, such as the Belgian Congo, the colonial power was described as the "state-entrepreneur." The state was at the same time investor as well as legal and political authority. Colonization thus gave rise to the bureaucratic state, initially composed of Europeans but from the 1930s onward increasingly Africanized. Government officials exercised both political and economic power. Collaboration between colonial administrators and managers of private companies was extremely close, to the point of blurring distinctions between public and private. Several of the participants in the colloquium focused on the role of the state apparatus in stimulating enterprises. A large portion of businesses establihsed during the colonial era were born and developed to satisfy the needs of the state. This is the legacy of the colonial experience which obtains in much of the Third World.

With the passing of the colonial era and the emergence of numerous bilateral and multilateral donor agencies involved in the development process, studies have been commissioned to ascertain the constraints to entrepreneurship in the Third World. There are contrasting views regarding the responsivenes of the supply of enterpreneurship over time. Economists have argued that the supply is responsive to market conditions, and that any deficiences are due either to market or policy imperfections.

They suggest that it is a "slack variable" and thus not a constraint to development. Others who focus on psychological and sociological theories of entrepreneurial supply are more pessimistic. They tend to look at ethnicity, status, and education as determinants of entrepreneurial supply.

Most of these studies have examined entrepreneurship in the larger, urban-based firms. Very few detailed studies of rural entrepreneurs have been conducted. Among those who have made the rural milieu the focus of their study are Enyinna Chuta and Carl Liedholm. In their review of the studies of entrepreneurial supply, Chuta and Liedholm conclude that there is generally a serious deficiency in the entrepreneur's managerial and technical performance in most countries. A crucial question then is whether or not the provision of training would overcome this constraint. They note that some authors see these shortcomings as "enduring impediments rooted in sociological variables," while others argue that appropriate training would be sufficient to overcome them. In this respect, Chuta and Liedholm suggest that there is little evidence to indicate that formal education and entrepreneurial success are related. Nonformal education may be a more relevant form of training for smaller rural entrepreneurs. In most rural areas the apprenticeship system is the primary vehicle for providing technical training. Business record keeping is a skill that can be acquired by non-formal methods, yet most rural entrepreneurs keep no records at all.

The nature of managerial and technical constraints on entrepreneurial supply tends to vary according to the type of business expansion involved. The supply of entrepreneurial services may be increased through an expansion of existing enterprises or by a proliferation of new ones. There is some evidence to show that there is deterioration in managerial performance as very small enterprises expand beyond the point where the owner can control everything himself. The type of training needed to overcome these problems would be different than that required for beginning firms. Finally, Chuta and Liedholm say that there is little empirical evidence to indicate how other socioeconomic factors affect the supply of rural entrepreneurs. The few existing studies generally have not been able to verify that sociological factors such as caste, ethnicity, and occupation of parents are important determinants of entrepreneurial supply. Clearly, those interested in promoting small and medium-scale enterprises need to support this type of research.

The Small Business Sector in the Third World

Small businesses with fewer than 100 employees account for more than half the industrial employment and a very large proportion of total production in the Third World. Surveys of small scale industries have shown that there are over 50 definitions of small business. Many countries have no official definition of small business, while others have several different definitions. They encompass sole proprietorships, family businesses, partnerships with a few workers, cottage industries, and artisans. Their contribution to development is substantial, even in the more advanced countries. For example, fully 87 percent of manufacturing employment in Indonesia and 70 percent in Colombia is accounted for by small enterprises.

Although large industries continue to absorb most of total investment, they still account for a small portion of industrial employment. Larger industries are concentrated in urban areas, whereas household or cottage industries are widely dispersed in provincial towns and rural areas and are usually more labor intensive. Household manufacturing comprises such enterprises as blacksmiths, shoemakers, garmentmakers, handcrafts, masons, carpenters, builders, and various crop-processing activities. Their function is primarily to provide inputs and processing services to agriculture and the non-food needs of the rural population. In earlier studies of these types of industries it was often thought that they were too traditional and economically backward to contribute to development.

Many of the books and articles written about small business in the developing world begin by noting how little is known about their actual performance. However, small and medium-scale industries are generally considered to play an important role in both income generation and employment creation. They are thought to have several advantages over large-scale industries:

● Small and medium-scale businesses are labor-intensive and use relatively simple techniques of production, which correspond with the abundance of labor and scarcity of capital in most developing countries;

● They are considered more efficient in the use of capital and in mobilizing savings, entrepreneurial talent, and other resources that would otherwise not be tapped;

● They can be useful suppliers to large industries and satisfy neglected demands more efficiently than big industries;

● Small businesses sometimes succeed by serving limited or specialized markets that are not attractive to larger industries;

57

● They are the seedbed of entrepreneurial talent and a testing place for new industries;

● They are more likely to enhance community stability than are big industries, whose interests may reach across regional and national borders;

● Small businesses are generally more capable of raising the level of popular participation in the economy.

There is a rather bewildering lexicon of terms and numbers of employees used to define small business (industry, enterprise) in the Third World. The role of small business in the development process has been the subject of numerous studies over the past 30 years. In general terms, large industries have been defined as having more than 100 employees, small industries less than 100, and household or cottage industries fewer than 10. The latter are variously refered to as micro-enterprises. In a recent study of the small and medium scale industries of ASEAN (Association of Southeast Asian Nations) Bruch and Hiemenz used the following, generally recognized, classification:

1-9 employees	cottage and household industries
10-49 employees	small-scale industries
50-99 employees	medium-scale industries
100 + employees	large-scale industries

The owner of a cottage industry is generally engaged in production and spends relatively little time on management. Employees are likely to be members of the family and contacts with the outside world are mostly informal. Small-scale industries are characterized by some division of labor, with the manager or entrepreneur not usually participating directly in the production process. In the medium-scale industries there is some formal organization of activities and specialization in management; in large-scale industries this pattern is the norm.

In their comparative survey of Asia, Bruch and Hiemenz examine some of the major features of small business in the Third World. Looking at plant size, they note that in nearly all countries, both industrialized and developing, a substantial part of manufacturing takes place in small and medium-scale enterprises. For example, in the United States about 70 percent of all businesses engaging five or more persons employed a total of fewer than 50 persons in 1972. The figures are even more striking for other industrialized countries. In most developing countries, businesses employing five to 49 persons account for fully 90 percent of all manufacturing firms with five or more persons. Even in highly industrialized countries, at least half of all manufacturing firms employ fewer than five persons.

Using their typologies of plant size noted above, Bruch and Hiemenz arrive at several general observations in the ASEAN countries. In Indonesia and the Philippines, cottage and household industries appear to be extremely important in terms of their employment shares, but much less important in Malaysia and Singapore. Cottage industries tend to be concentrated mainly in the food, furniture and pottery industries, as measured by their employment shares. Other industries with a relatively high share of employment in this sector are clothing, footwear, leather, and wood and metal products. However, cottage industries are virtually nonexistent in the production of tobaocco products, industrial chemicals, basic metals, electrical machinery, and professional goods. As might be expected, in all the ASEAN countries, large industries prevail in "modern" industries characterized by economies of scale, such as the production of electrical machinery, transport equipment, and rubber, glass, and tobacco products.

Regarding contribution to employment, output, and income generation, the authors maintain that the unsatisfactory growth performance of small and medium-scale industries in most ASEAN countries calls for a more rigorous analysis of the relative importance of size. The proposed analysis would seek to assess whether small and medium-scale industries have been less suited to serve development objectives than have larger firms. Among ASEAN countries, the manufacturing sector of Indonesia is the most heterogeneous in terms of establishment characteristics. The highly informal nature of these micro-enterprises is revealed in the fact that less than five percent of workers in firms with up to four employees are paid. These are generally either household industries or small workshops depending upon family labor. In somewhat larger cottage industries (five to nine workers), about three-quarters of all workers are paid employees. The share steadily increases with plant size. Many cottage industries do not operate continuously during the whole year.

Compared with Indonesia and the Philippines, the Malaysian manufacturing sector is far less structurally heterogeneous. Very small firms with fewer than ten employees show a considerably higher degree of formal organization. They operate on twice as many days per year as those of similar size in Indonesia. Capital intensity is increasing, with plant sizes of up to 250 employees. Capital-intensive industries employing more than 500 workers in electronics and textiles in Malaysia are due to foreign direct investment. This is even more pronounced in Singapore, where capital intensity is greatest in firms with up to 300 employees.

Obstacles to Small Business Development

Small businesses in the developing world face some rather overwhelming obstacles. Many of the problems faced in the Third World environment bear a resemblance to those we have identified in the United States, particularly regarding access to credit. While there are numerous problems facing small businesses, the major ones may be summarized as follows:

● They lack access to institutional credit and government facilities;

● They lack technical and marketing assistance, often depending upon middlemen and moneylenders;

● One person is often responsible for such functions as production, administration, finance, and marketing, which are distributed among several persons in a large business.

These problems must be viewed in the context of economic policies in many developing countries that stand in direct contradiction to efforts at assisting small industries. Often government policies show a preference for capital-intensive rather than labor intensive industries. Government policies often favor large local and foreign-based businesses rather than small local industries. Many of the examples frequently cited to illustrate these problems sound remarkably similar to those faced by small businesses in the United States:

● The tariffs and investment incentives are often expressly intended to foster large-scale industry;

● Administrative controls on interest rates, as well as the borrowings and lendings of the organized financial sector make it more profitable for intermediaries to lend to large (often foreign owned) companies;

● Even when finance has been made available to small businesses, it has found its way to influencial borrowers of good standing rather than to new entrepreneurs;

● Agricultural policies which restrict the growth of rural incomes also restrict the markets for the products of small-scale local industries.

Under the heading of policies resulting in factor price distortions, Chuta and Liedholm list those government policies which affect rural enterprises. In most instances, they apply to small enterprises in general.

● **Interest rates.** Two distinct capital markets exist in most developing countries: "formal" and "informal." Banks and other institutions constitute the formal market, while the informal market consists of money lenders and raw materials suppliers. Interest rates vary widely between the two. Typically, official rates - with government imposed ceilings - range from nine to 24 percent, whereas the non-official rates range from 29 to 200 percent. The official rate in Thailand, for example, was only 9 percent in 1973, compared with a non-official rate of 29 percent. In Colombia, the official rate was 24 percent in 1974, compared with a non-official rate of 36 to 60 percent. Under inflationary conditions the formal real rates become quite low, sometimes negative. Banks therefore tend to lend to only the established, large-scale businesses, involving lower risks and lending costs. Clients are usually urban-based and capital-intensive.

● **Tariffs.** Import duties often favor large urban industries over small rural enterprises. In general, import duties are lowest for heavy capital goods and become progressively higher through intermediate and consumer durable goods categories. But many items classified as intermediate or consumer goods in tariff schedules are capital goods for rural small-scale firms. In Sierra Leone, for example, the sewing machine is classified as a luxury consumer good and taxed accordingly, even though it is an important capital item for tailors. Sometimes a total waiver of import duties is granted on capital goods or raw materials for specified periods to induce industrial development. Even though small firms may qualify for the waiver, they may be unaware of the opportunity or find the process of applying too complex and time-consuming. It should also be noted that tariffs can bring direct benefit to rural enterprises when placed on commodities they produce.

● **Foreign Exchange.** Often governments in the Third World maintain a high price for foreign exchange but grant concessionary rates to large firms. Small firms are deprived of the same advantages since they do not qualify for the concessional rates or do not know about them. In any case, large firms usually import relatively more equipment and therefore benefit more than small firms. As a result, foreign exchange policies tend to encourage greater capital intensity among urban large-scale industries. When foreign exchange is rationed the larger firms are more likely to have access to these scarce resources.

● **Other Tax Incentives.** Many governments employ tax incentives to encourage industrial development. These include tax holiday periods, accelerated depreciation and investment allowances, and exemptions from import duties. They provide an advantage to those firms that qualify, which usually means the larger ones. Often the requirements are so complicated and time

61

consuming that they discourage small-scale entrepreneurs. By the
same token, the smaller enterprises often are either exempted
from paying income taxes or the government is ineffective at collecting them. Sales and excise taxes which apply at all stages
in the production process fall more heavily on small firms.

● Minimum Wage Regulations. Minimum wage policies are used
in the attempt to achieve social equity. They usually apply to
larger enterprises in the urban areas, but even when they are
applied in the rural areas they are often not effectively enforced among small firms. The net effect, however, is to encourage rural to urban migration, depriving rural enterprises of
potential workers as well as entrepreneurs.

Chuta and Liedholm also outline policies other than those
which affect prices:

● Infrastructure. There are government policies intended
to develop the infrastructure of the economy that may affect
small enterprises. These have to do with the provision of electricity, water, or roads, advantages which may benefit large and
small firms alike. Small firms do not usually require large
amounts of costly infrastructure, as do larger firms. In the case
of electricity, initially installations may be small generating
units for selected enterprises, followed by larger generators
serving several enterprises, and eventually a community-wide service for all.

● Industrial Policies. Some policies, designed with large
urban firms in mind, also apply to small firms and work a hardship on them. Licenses or permits to engage in business may be
so exacting and time-consuming that they intimidate the small
entrepreneur. In recognition of the this problem, some countries
such as India have taken measures to reserve certain business
activities to small-scale firms. Brazil has attempted to make the
licensing process more accessible to small firms. Conditions of
employment and product standards specified by the government may
also be obstacles for small firms. These regulations can have
both positive and negative effects on consumers as well as the
firm and its employees. Health and saftey standards help to
safeguard workers, for example.

Another category of policies are those affecting the demand
for the products of rural enterprises. Since agriculture generates the largest share of rural income, it is clear that
policies designed to increase agricultural production will have
an impact on the demand for rural non-farm activities. Pricing
policies that improve the terms of trade between agricultural and
the large-scale urban sector affect agricultural production and
farm income. The type of policies implemented will determine who
benefits within the rural community. Such farm implements as

62

tractors and fertilizers are more apt to be used by large-scale farmers and are less likely to be produced in rural areas than are those implements used by small-scale farmers. Hence, those policies designed to benefit a larger number of small-scale, low income farmers are likely to generate a greater demand for rural enterprises and services than those designed to benefit a few large-scale farmers. Government policies to favor sub-contracting of small firms with larger firms may help to stimulate industrial linkages and thus benefit small firms.

Obstacles to entrepreneurship in the Third World are becoming the subject of interest to scholars and journalists, as well as policy-makers anxious to push every button available to start the development engine. Jeune Afrique Economique devoted an issue to the African entrepreneur, now becoming the object of a gamble to stimulate national investment. African nations are turning to the indigenous entrepreneur with their hopes of industrialization, which have floundered with other strategies of development. The image of the entrepreneur in Africa that emerges from this special issue is that of the first generation of "self-made men" who have pulled themselves up by their own boot straps against great odds.

But the obstacles to be overcome by African entrepreneurs are daunting. They are typically not from business families as in western countries. They are most often men and women who come from the working class, usually having served several years of apprenticeship. They have had little chance to save money to begin their own business. Extended family financial obligations are usually such that anyone who starts to get ahead is subject to requests for assistance. On the other hand, a typical African entrepreneur is likely to have received an initial loan from some member of the extended family.

The typical rural African enterprise develops in a rather hostile environment. Many of the problems are not directly related to government policies described above, but to the general conditions of life in the rural areas. In spite of its rich artisanal heritage, Africa has been slow to master industrial technology. African enterpreneurs have little capital with which to begin a business. They lack qualified employees, especially in the rural areas, because young people are drawn to the cities to look for work. Even if an industry reaches the level of 15 to 50 workers, the chain of production often remains rudimentary. Human labor is preferred to machines since this is the source of value added. Many rural enterprises are thus forced to remain at the artisanal stage, using few machines, with no electricity, and resulting in poor rates of productivity.

One economic fact of life limits the growth of even those African enterprises that manage to resolve these problems. It has to do with the weak purchasing power of the African consumer and the usually narrow national market. In only a handful of African countries such as Nigeria is there a substantial concentration of population. In order to expand, a local enterprise must look beyond its borders for markets. The per capita income among African countries ranges from $180 to $1500, compared with $10,000 to $15,000 in the industrial countries. A very small portion of the population - usually between 5 and 25 percent - are wage earners who have a regular income. The income of farmers and artisans in the rural areas is subject to the vagaries of weather which affects crop production. And these people make up the vast majority of the population.

Competition among small firms at the local level is fierce. Little data is available on the mortality rate among new enterprises, but it is fair to assume that the rate of small enterprise failures in the developing world is at least the equivalent of those in developed economies. Small firms are forced to wage prices wars just to stay in business. This in turn accounts for the frequently low quality of products.

The search for export markets is complicated by a number of factors. In spite of much rhetoric regarding the necessity of achieving regional economic integration, the tendency of most African governments has been to look out for number one. Protectionism remains the order of the day. Industrial cooperation among African nations has a tortured history, replete with failed attempts. For small and medium sized local industries, competition in the export market is severe. This is because, as we have seen, foreign owned companies (multinationals) continue to hold the lion's share of the domestic market. They dominate both through exports of their own products and by implanting powerful local affiliates. They benefit from investment codes designed by governments anxious to attract foreign capital and thus achieve rapid industrial growth. Hence, local initiative is stifled by government policies which, in many cases, were designed 20 years ago.

One of the chief handicaps to the development of African enterprises is the lack of good management. Although there is now a small and growing cadre of young Africans who have entered the market with undergraduate and graduate degrees in business administration, they lack practical experience. The self-made African entrepreneur who has started a business alone is often reluctant to delegate responsibility and authority to a young MBA graduate acquainted with modern managerial techniques. The proprietor is most apt to confound creating a business with managing it. The temptation is to centralize decision-making authority, attending to even the smallest details of management rather than delegating responsibility. This is likely to include his signature on the slightest disbursement of funds.

The African enterprise frequently functions without even an elementary notion of financial accounting. And when a decision is made to set up an accounting system after the first flush of success, it is too late. Often as not, the African entrepreneur views the professional accountant as more of a spy than a trusted financial advisor. The consequences of neglecting financial accounting for a growing firm can be disastrous. Without cost calculations and sales projections, the business may continue to set unrealistic prices on its products. The owner is also tempted to confuse the business with his own personal property, thinking nothing of dipping into profits in order to settle personal debts, pay a child's school fees, or repair the house.

Nevetheless, there is a growing awareness of the need to adapt modern managerial techniques to traditional African values. African enterprise and the professional manager are taking the place of ethnographies and political systems as the most popular subjects of research. Adaptations to the African milieu may entail the manager's ignoring formal lines separating management and workers in European systems. For example, African managers surveyed about their relations with workers indicated that it is not unusual for them to take a sick worker to the hospital and to assist his family out of his own pocket. Formal hierarchical relations within the company may be short-circuited by informal family ties which take precedence. A "patron" may not simply be a direct superior within the company but someone from the same village or region.

Today the African manager is more and more likely to have studied at an American business school. Those trained abroad still constitute an elite minority. Increasingly, the degree in business management from an American university is becoming the standard by which others are measured. This contrasts with the value of diplomas in other disciplines, where European degrees often remain the standard and American degrees still come out on the short end of the equivalency issue.

Overcoming a Key Obstacle: Small-Scale Bank Lending

Numerous studies have suggested that inadequate credit is one of the principal obstacles facing most small businesses in developing countries. In 1984 Jason Brown conducted a comparative analysis of small-scale bank lending in nine countries. While pointing out that the data are quite uneven, he concludes that few of these businesses are receiving credit from any formal lending institutions. Rather, most small business lending world wide is provided by friends and relatives and, to a lesser extent, by informal sources such as money lenders.

65

Brown points out that there is some disagreement among experts on the extent to which this concern of businesses with credit represents a genuine need, as opposed to a misapplication of existing sources of capital. But no one has concluded that the increased availability of credit is not an important element in business expansion. Just as in the industrialized countries, banks and other formal lending institutions have been slow to respond to the credit needs of small businesses. A major reason is related to the difficulty in handling a large number of small accounts at an acceptable cost. In cases where there have been successful attempts at small-scale lending, such as in India and the Philippines, government policy has provided a stimulus. Some governments have required that a certain percentage of the value of loan funds be utilized for development purposes.

Lending to small businesses is being carried out by a wide variety of banking-type institutions in developing countries. Chief among them are cooperative banks, which are typically developed to complement other services provided to farmers. Other institutions are established and managed by governments to achieve specific objectives. For example, the Badan Kredit Kecamatan (BKK) in Indonesia was set up by the provincial and central governments to provide credit to small businesses. But the main non-family source of small-scale lending to business is money lenders. They may charge interest rates as high as 100 percent a day, but average five to 20 percent a day for urban vendors. The rates may seem exploitative, but they do reflect the high risk associated with such lending. Some countries such as India have experimented with providing bank lending to money lenders at low rates in an effort to cushion the risk and enable the lenders to pass on lower rates to borrowers. It remains to be seen how successul this approach will be.

There are also lending institutions run by voluntary, non-profit, organizations. Most of them are cooperatives tied to farmer groups. Some banks are interested in using these groups as a low-cost way to identify and supervise borrowers. This has been accomplished with some success in India and Kenya, and is likely to be tried in other countries.

The size of small-scale loans varies from bank to bank and country to country. The average loan of the Badan Kredit Kecamatan in Indonesia is $50.00. Small-scale lending represents on the average less than five percent of total loaned funds of commercial banks. Other small-scale lending programs with signi-ficant loan volume, such as those in El Salvador, are not oper-ated by commercial banks but by government institutions. This indicates that the impetus for small-scale lending has been mainly political.

Several generalizations emerge from Brown's study of small-scale lending in developing countries:

● Policy environment. According to Brown, no single factor has been more significant in the emergence of these programs than the policy environment. India provides the most compelling example. Millions of loans have been made to date, almost entirely due to government policy. Larger programs exist only where there were clear incentives at the beginning. Flexible interest rate ceilings are also a factor. Where they are rigidly enforced below true market rates, programs tend not to grow, regardless of other incentives.

● Profitability. The most critical and most elusive issue is profitability. Many of the factors which contribute to profitability of loans to small businesses are well known. Brown suggests that on the basis of observations in several Asian countries, banks should view small-scale lending as a means for tapping new markets. Banks should also see it as a possible source of profit, espcially if interest rates are not unreasonably controlled and loan volume can be increased.

● Use of intermediaries. Brown found much interest among banks in the greater use of intermediaries such as non-profit organizations and money lenders to distribute credit. USAID and other donors are funding projects which are experimenting in this area. Generally, successful use of non-profit intermediaries has occurred where the organizations were fairly large and well-organized. Alternative intermediaries could be money lenders, even though they often have an unsavory reputation. Many banks already provide commercial credit to money lenders, who usually have collateral and repay on time.

● The role of banks and the issue of subsidy. This is another weighty question. Many economists would argue that the only way to reach large numbers of small borrowers efficiently worldwide is through commercial banks which provide unsubsidized credit. But large successful government programs such as the BKK in Indonesia and the Dominican Republic would appear to refute this argument since they are not run by commercial banks. The question is whether the establishment of a subsidized, non-commercial bank program is the most efficient use of resources.

Commercial banks are in the business of dispensing credit and have established networks to do so. The main problem is in getting them to start lending in this sector. This is when a subsidy makes sense. Banks may need various short-term subsidies to start up a small-scale loan program, but then they should operate it profitably on their own.

Brown concludes that lending at this level in developing countries is in fact growing very rapidly. Banks are overcoming their fears and finding ways to make such loans at acceptable costs, for whatever economic and political reason. The key to a successful program, he believes, is the commitment to undertake small-scale lending in a big way. Although the risks seem to outweigh the advantages initially, Brown contends that the case studies show that small-scale lending to businesses can lead to substantial new markets and eventually to profits.

Public Policy and Small Business Development

At the time of political independence in the late 1950s and early 1960s, the attitude toward indigenous entrepreneurs ranged between hostility and benign neglect. Many Third World nations opted for strategies of development which placed emphasis on capital-intensive industrial development, relying upon the state as the engine of growth. Those nations which embraced the ideology of Marxism were generally hostile to the promotion of national entrepreneurs. The revolutionary ideology espoused by Third World spokesmen such as Franz Fanon strongly opposed the development of a national "bourgeoisie." National political leaders such as Julius Nyerere lamented their nation's lack of "citizens who have sufficient capital to establish modern industries."

The attitude of those leaders who chose to follow a mixed economy approach to development was scarcely more favorably disposed toward their "local capitalists." In their rush toward industrial growth, they were more inclined to devise liberal investment codes to lure foreign investors than to promote local industries.

The example of two African countries considered to be models of capitalist development is the subject of a study by an African scholar. Mushi Mugumorhagerwa examined the cases of the Ivory Coast and Kenya in a doctoral disseration. He concluded that although both governments have professed commitment to indigenous entrepreneurial participation in the economy, they manifest a similar underlying spirit "relatively biased against genuine indigenous entrepreneurship. Entrepreneurial promotion is subordinated to other development goals such as the creation of employment and regional decentralization of the economy."

Mushi maintains that the indifference of the state in situations of conflict between local industries and foreign capital works against the control of the economy by nationals. Premature mobilitzation of indigenous capital specifically for development purposes and the caution prompted by the need to protect collective interests may not even lead to promotion of social equity.

In his comparative study of Kenya and the Ivory Coast, Mushi notes that their entrepreneurial programs differ sharply. Kenya has combined financial and technical assistance through the industrial estates approach. Its program is much wider and more differentiated, including small rural loan schemes with the rural industrial estates. Established in 1968, the Kenya Industrial Estates Limited is devoted to a set of goals: assisting entrepreneurs in all aspects of industry formation and management, helping the government to formulate appropriate policies, and implementing a program of industrial promotion centers.

By contrast, the Ivory Coast has yet to develop an effective policy of assisting local entrepreneurs. It has followed a more minimalist approach to government involvement, relying on a formula of assistance to privately managed lending institutions. The government simply seeks to minimize the costs which banking institutions may incur as a result of lending to unsuccessful entrepreneurs. The result of this policy has been the development of a few large-scale enterprises owned by Ivorians and the flourishing of joint ventures controlled in majority by expatriates. The economy is noticeably lacking in medium-sized enterprises owned and operated by nationals.

The relations between the state and indigenous entrepreneurs in Cameroon has been the subject of study by a Cameroonian scholar, Wilfred Ndongko. Today Cameroon is among a handful of African countries that have followed a well-documented and relatively successful path of economic development. At the time of independence in 1960, Cameroon was considered among the least developed economies on the continent, with modest chances for growth. Now it is regarded as a middle income country and among the safest countries in the Third World for foreign investment. The country has managed to maintain an impressive political stability, which has contributed to its healthy business climate. The Cameroonian experience has especially attracted attention in recent years, in light of the disappointing performance of the Ivory Coast and Kenya, heretofore considered to be Africa's "success stories."

By 1983, after the economies of Kenya and the Ivory Coast had started their decline, the Cameroonian economy was still growing at a rate of six percent in real terms. Production was well diversified and foreign exchange was being earned from a wide array of goods. Remarkably, the 1983 budget was balanced, solely financed from Cameroonian resources without any foreign borrowing. However, as Ndongko observes in his study, in spite of stated government policies to promote indigenous entrepreneurs, foreign capital still plays a dominant role. Although the economy has witnessed a successful period of economic growth since independence, largely because of the government's policy of planned liberalism which encourages private sector initiatives, an independent indigenous entrepreneurial class has yet to emerge.

The state's intervention in the economy has generally favored large-scale foreign enterprises. Some national entrepreneurs have been successful in commercial retailing and urban real estate. But import and distributive trade sectors are still dominated by foreign capital. The handful of Cameroonian entrepreneurs who have established large-scale industries have done so in association with foreign partners or the state. Reviewing the history of economic development and government policy since independence, Ndongko concludes that opportunities for local entrepreneurs to accumulate capital and play a key role in industrialization have not been present.

At the time of independence Cameroon had a small open economy, with foreign trade accounting for more than 25 percent of the national product. Export trade was characterized by heavy dependence upon a few primary agricultural commodities such as cocoa, coffee, tea, palm oil, and cotton. By 1980, petroleum products accounted for 27 percent of total exports and agricultural products comprised just over half. There were few inter-industry links since the bulk of the processing of exportable agricultural surplus was carried out in Europe. The repatriated earnings of foreign capital exceeded the inflow of new resources into the country. As a result, Cameroonian businesses were unable to develop independently of foreign investors.

The Cameroonian government sought to increase the supply of capital to nascent local industries through a variety of institutional and legislative instruments. They were intended to provide local businesses with more decentralized and better technical assistance in business management. An investment code provided preferential treatment in such areas as duty-free entry of certain raw materials, tax exemptions, and investments in sectors deemed important to the country's long-term development. However, the effect of the investment code has generally been a very modest participation by nationals in the formation of capital for industrial enterprises because of the high foreign exchange costs they would incur.

Credit facilities for local enterprises have been greatly expanded in a conscious effort by the state to develop domestic capital. Several public institutions have been created for this purpose. These include the National Investment Corporation (SNI), the Cameroon Development Bank (BCD), the National Fund for Rural Development, (FONADER), the National Centre for the Assistance of Small and Medium-Sized Enterprises (CAPME), and the Aid and Loan Fund Guarantee Fund to Small and Medium-Sized Enterprises (FOGAPE). (All are known by their francophone acronyms.) While each of these institutions is meant to make capital available to small businesses, the results have not always been those antici-

70

pated. For example, most of the enterprises in which SNI has
shares are running at a loss. This is due in part to the ineffi-
cient management of parastatal enterprises.

During the 1970s, there was a push toward the expansion of
these state credit institutions. The BCD is the source of government financing to local commercial and industrial firms and is
funded almost entirely from government sources. Its objective is
to support all local enterprises, although particular attention
has been given to small and medium-sized firms. FONADER is an agricultural credit bank which provides credit to farmers as part
of development projects. FOGAPE assists local traders and entrepreneurs who do not have access to other established credit
facilities.

A practitioner of small enterprise development, Gary Kilmer
of Development Alternatives, Inc., has described the policy environment for enterprise development in Central Java where he worked. He describes the system of incentives and restrictions set
up by the government of Indonesia as very complex. There is a
wide array of organizations to implement policy aimed at achieving the objective of balanced and stable economic growth with
equity. Kilmer notes that the policy environment has been
studied by several analysts who maintain that the government has
done more to control and restrict enterprise development than to
promote it. Other researchers who have examined particular aspects of government policy have tended to conclude that the most
serious problem is the uncertainty among entrepreneurs about the
complexity of government regulations and the system of informal
payments (punggli) that has developed to overcome bureaucratic
obstacles.

Kilmer reports that obtaining interview data from entrepreneurs about the real impact of government policies on their business was very difficult. They seemed accustomed to the policy
environment as it exists and tended not to reflect on ways in
which it could be improved. On the basis of the information he
was able to obtain, however, Kilmer provides observations on such
policy areas as credit and finance, licensing, taxation, and
trade.

The financial system in Indonesia has been characterized as
a tool for transferring government funds to certain types of economic activities rather than as a means for integrating capital
markets and moving privately held investment capital from surplus
to deficit areas. This is reflected in the key role which state-
owned banks play in the economy, and the degree to which their
lending portfolios are dominated by subsidized lending programs
financed by the central government. All government sponsored and
financed lending programs are subsidized, and interest rates are

71

controlled at between 10.5 and 13 percent. The main form of subsidy is a low-cost rediscount facility (three to six percent) from the Bank of Indonesia for loans made under government programs. Thus, the banks are not forced to go to the market place or pay market rates for their funds. They simply lend at the rates mandated by the various government programs. According to Kilmer, these programs have been very effective in transferring large amounts of investment funds to small-scale entrepreneurs. But there are other impacts whose implications must be noted.

The bulk of bank resources are placed in the easiest investments with the highest possible short-term return. In Central Java, low cost credit encourages the development of activities in the trade and service sectors rather than in the manufacturing sector. Subsidized credit programs also distort the local capital market by establishing a cost of capital which is not based on demand. This leads to excess demand for loan capital which cannot be satisfied by existing programs. This situation is reflected in the system of informal payments which borrowers must make to bank officials in order to have their applications considered.

Licensing requirements in Indonesia are extremely complex and subject to interpretation at all levels of government. As might be expected, then, most of the problems related to licensing arise from the large number of agencies that interpret the regulations. One obvious problem is that of the uncertainty on the part of the entrepreneur as to what is really required of him or her. There is no clear means of communicating all of the various regulations. Nor is there a single body responsible for monitoring compliance with the regulations

Tax policy in Indonesia affecting the enterprise development process may be divided into three categories: company tax, personal income tax, and sales tax. Although in all of these areas policy guidelines are clearly laid out, the government manages to generate a very small portion of its revenues from these sources. Enforcement of the policies is quite variable and leads to uncertainty among taxpayers as to how much they are actually liable to pay. These uncertainties leave the small-scale entrepreneur in particular subject to negotiating his income tax bill with the tax authorities. The system leaves open the possibility of payoffs to the tax official in exchange for a low estimation of annual profits and hence a low estimate of the amount of taxes due.

Until the devaluation of 1978, Indonesia's international trade policy was based mainly upon import substitution and the protection of local industries. The policy was very successful in encouraging the development of an industrial base in Indonesia. But it also resulted in serious inefficiencies in resource mobilization and price distortions, and in some cases produced the opposite effect intended by the government. For example, the encouragement of capital intensive production technologies was not conducive to achieving another important goal: increasing employment opportunities.

After the devaluation, the thrust of government trade policy began to shift toward the promotion of growth in non-oil exports. This included an effort to lower the import trade barriers in some instances. The program was relatively successful in expanding the export of non-oil products until 1982, when the situation was reversed with the deepening of the worldwide recession and the sharp decline in demand for Indonesian goods. This trend is likely to continue unless there is substantial improvement in the world economy.

In July 1985, the government of Indonesia signed an historic agreement to begin trading with the People's Republic of China for the first time in nearly two decades. Both sides acknowledged that the memorandum of understanding was a major breakthrough in relations between the two countries. Indonesia suspended relations with Peking in 1967, two years after crushing a communist-led coup which the Indonesian government claimed had Chinese support. There will still be no diplomatic relations with China, according to Indonesian President Suharto, until China formally states that it will not support communist movements in the region. Indonesia's exports to China in 1983 were valued at about $33.5 million annually, while China's exports to Indonesia via Hong Kong amounted to $208 million.

Conclusion

In this chapter the economies of the Third World and the role of small business in the development process have been examined. This entailed an inquiry into the nature of the entrepreneur in developing countries and the rather awesome problems which small-scale enterprises face. It is clear that there is now a renewed awareness and appreciation of the potential which small and medium sized enterprises carry for development. Third World governments are beginning to fashion policies designed to stimulate this sector by providing credit and technical assistance. They must also consider ways of minimizing the effect of those policies which impede the development of new businesses, especially in the area of licensing and other regulations.

A policy agenda that might provide a more conducive environment for small business in the developing world would include the following elements:

● <u>Credit</u>. This is one of the most commonly expressed needs
among small-scale entrepreneurs. The availability of credit can
be increased by increasing or removing interest rate ceilings
which make it profitable to established banks to lend to small
businesses. But there is also a need to increase the number and
range of institutions which dispense credit, especially those
that can reach the smaller enterprises that have heretofore been
out of the formal credit market.

● <u>Technical assistance</u>. Business advisory services are
sorely needed at all levels, but especially for those new businesses just getting started. This includes providing instruc-
tion in basic accounting and financial management, as well as
market surveys, inventory, and pricing. Programs can be establish so that the providing agency or consulting firm charge fees
for their services.

● <u>Increasing Markets</u>. Unfair competition in the form of subsidies provided to large-scale enterprises should be eliminated.
The demand for products and services of small firms would be
increased by removing the barriers to the trading companies which
market them. Governments can ensure that small firms benefit
from import duty rebates or exemptions on raw materials, just as
large firms do. Markets for small firms can also be enlarged by
providing for sub-contracting arrangements on government contracts for maintenance and repair services.

● <u>Human Resources</u>. Government policies can provide for increased labor skills by supplementing existing on-the-job training. Government vocational training programs can be adapted to
the needs of small businesses. Advice and assistance in training
can best by provided by the suppliers and customers of small
businesses.

● <u>Licensing and Regulations</u>. Some governments have already
taken steps to remove the barriers that complex licensing and
regulations represent, especially to smaller firms. This allows
more small firms to come in out of the informal sector and to
benefit from the range of services available to legitimate
businesses.

74

Chapter Three References

Jeune Afrique Economique, "Entrepreises Africaines: 700 Leaders"
     (Classement 1984), special edition, December 1984.

Ray Bromley (ed), Planning for Small Enerprises in Third World
     Cities, New York: Pergmon Press, 1985, pp. 321-341.

Francisco de Oliveira, "A Critique of Dualist Reason: the Brazil-
     ian Economy Since 1930", in Bromley, cited above, pp. 65-95.

Ray Brown, Indigenous Enterprises in Less Developed Countries:
     The Importance of Entrepreneurs to the Development
     Process, PhD disseration, Clarement Graduate School,
     1982.

Catherine Coquery-Vidrovitch, introduction to Entreprises et
     Entrepreneurs en Afrique: XIXe et XXe Siecles, (Tome I),
     Paris: l'Harmattan, 1983; collection of papers presented
     at a colloquium held under auspices of Agence de Coopera-
     tion Culturelle et Technique.

Enyinna Chuta and Carl Liedholm, Rural Non-Farm Employment:
     A Review of the State of the Art, Michigan State Univ-
     ersity, Department of Agricultural Economics, Paper No. 4
     of Rural Development series, 1979.

Keith Marsden, "Creating the Right Environment for Small Firms,"
     in Economic Development and the Private Sector,
     World Bank, 1983, pp. 13-16.

Mathias Bruch and Ulrich Hiemenz, Small and Medium-Scale
     Industires in the ASEAN Countries: Agents or Victims of
     Economic Development?, Boulder, Colo.: Westview Press,
     1984.

Dennis Anderson, Small Industry in Developing Countries: Some
     Issues, World Bank Staff Working Paper No. 518, 1982.

Catherine Some, "Regards sur l'Entreprise Africaine," in Jeune
     Afrique Economique, December 1984, pp. 27-37.

Jason Brown, "Small-Scale Bank Lending in Developing Countries:
     A Comparative Analysis," paper prepared for AID, Office
     of Rural and Institutional Development, Bureau for
     Science and Technology, April 1984.

75

Mushi   Mugumorhagerwa, "African Governments and Indigenous Industrial Entrepreneurship: The Cases of Kenya and Ivory Coast," paper presented at the African Studies Association Meeting in Washington, D.C., November 1982.

Wilfred Ndongko, "The Political Economy of Development in Cameroon: Relations Between the State, Indigenous Businessmen, and Foreign Investors," paper presented at the Johns Hopkins School of Advanced International Studies, Washington, D.C., April 1984.

Gary Kilmer, "The Policy Environment for Enterprise Development in Central Java," Washington, D.C.: Development Alternatives, Inc., February 1983.

Chapter Four

Small Business and Development Assistance

"The presence and value of an indigenous private sector in developing countries need enhanced recognition. The private sectors' role in development has not been well explored and its dynamics are still too little understood......This is strange because the private sector generates almost three-quarters of the gross domestic product of developing countries."

- A.W. Clausen, World Bank President
Speech delivered February 26, 1985

In a speech to a group of British business executives in February 1985, World Bank President A.W. Clausen remarked that it was strange that the role of the private sector in development was the least discussed of all major development issues. Over the past two to three decades the thrust of development efforts has been directed toward public sector activities. Aid organizations have been less concerned with promoting private sector growth than with assisting the development of an effective public sector. Clausen added that this emphasis has been misplaced. Also misplaced, he said, was the tendency in international conferences to focus narrowly on the behavior of multinational corporations and foreign investors.

Clausen then proceded to suggest that the indigenous private sector in developing countries should be given increased recognition. The private sector role in development has not been well explored and its dynamics are not well understood. Focusing his attention on Africa, Clausen sought to refute the notion that there was a shortage of indigenous entrepreneurs, even though the public sector predominates in most African countries. The entrepreneurial spirit is there, but it is damped by barriers and distortions created by policymakers.

These are themes that have come to be commonplace among donor agencies. Indeed both bilateral and multilateral aid agencies are fashioning a whole new vocabulary with which to describe their mission. It is quite likely that we have entered a new era in which the issues in development assistance center, not so much on public versus private sector development, but on what types of private sector assistance are most effective. As is usually the case, the rhetoric of change has thus far outpaced effective programs of action. With this in mind, it is well to place efforts to stimulate private sector development in historical perspective.

United States Assistance to Small Business Development

United States foreign aid encompasses a broad range of programs that includes short-term military and political assistance to developing countries as well as economic assistance. Only a small portion of the total actually targets development. The Reagan administration's aid proposal for fiscal 1986 totalled $14.8 billion, of which only $2 billion was for long-term economic development. Rep. David R. Obey (D-Wis), Chairman of the House Appropriations Subcommittee on Foreign Operations, has observed that the $2 billion is so scattered worldwide that it is "virtually invisible." If this may be said of development assistance in general, it is especially so with respect to programs aimed at private sector developments and small businesses in particular. Indeed, one must say that these efforts have heretofore been largely symbolic.

Official U.S. promotion of small and medium scale industry in developing countries preceeded establishment of a formal assistance agency. One of the first efforts was in the Philippines, beginning in 1906. It involved crafts and raw materials production in the secondary school curriculum. Then, after the Second World War, the U.S. and United Nations agencies were asked to provide a variety of technical skills for cottage industries producing crafts for export. Even today crafts have maintained an important place in Philippine exports. In Latin America, U.S. assistance to small-scale industry preceeded the Marshall Plan for post World War II European rehabilitation. Assistance to the private sector was channeled through the Institute for Inter-American Development.

The legislative history of U.S. foreign assistance has been generally supportive of private enterprise in developing countries. This has included inducements such as support for feasibility studies by U.S. companies, small grants to firms in developing countries for food market exploration, and insurance against expropriation of the properties of U.S. companies. However, the insurance feature of foreign assistance for the most part has been relatively capital intensive and often oriented to import substitution. During the early years of emphasis on the industrialization in developing countries, AID and its predecessor agencies provided a variety of assistance to urban industrial programs. This included industrial advisors posted to government ministries, financial advisors to small firms, and loans to financial institutions.

There were two notable efforts to promote rural small-scale enterprise. The first was the Rural Industrialization Technical Assistance (RITA) Program in Northeast Brazil. Five projects involving U.S. universities were launched in 1964. The universities provided two or three professors and six to eight graduate students who gathered data on possible enterprise opportunities. Plans for each promising enterprise were prepared and mangers chosen for each one. During the life of the project 15 firms entered production and another 20 were in various stages of planning at the end of it. The projects included investment of $1550 for a shoe factory and $16,000 for a a corn processing plant. At the time of these projects there was general opposition to labor intensive ventures.

A second USAID effort was the Indigenous Industrial Development Project which operated in Nigeria from 1962 through 1971. Working through the Small Industries Division of the Federal Ministry of Industry, USAID assisted in the establishment of two Industrial Development Centers, one at Zaria and the other at Owerri. The goal of the project was to help small industries in starting, expanding, or improving their operations through the centers. Five major small industries were chosen for concentration: woodworking, metalworking, auto repair, textiles, and leatherworking. Assistance was provided to technical, management, and accounting aspects of business development.

The centers were to consist of offices and mechnical shops, both to be used for demonstration and training. The entrepreneurs were to receive training also at their business location. They were to be shown new production techniques, the use of new kinds of machinery, how to make new products, and how to keep books and manage the business. They were then to carry out independently what they had learned from the Center. The Centers were to be staffed with U.S. technicians and one or more Nigerian counterparts.

During the early stages of the project at the Owerri Center there were six U.S. advisors, including Peace Corps Volunteers. At the peak of operations there were about 40 Nigerian personnel. The entrepreneur seminars and demonstrations of new products and processes were developed in the following manner. First, teams of Nigerian and U.S. advisors visited the field to locate and meet with entrepreneurs. Other entrepreneurs were referred to the Center by government officials working in the area. School heads and trade school associated personnel also referred some of their students who were trying to start businesses or improve existing ones.

The Ford Foundation made a major contribution to the development of the project by providing credit. Nigerian counterparts were trained in financial management and a small number of loans were made with Foundation seed money. In June 1967, civil war broke out in Nigeria. The Owerri Center unit was closed and its advisors were all transferred to the Zaria Center in the north. Cooperation between the USAID and Foundation projects increased, however, and by 1970 the credit function was integrated into the Industrial Development Center.

By the end of USAID involvement in the project in 1972, over 2800 Nigerians had received training. One interesting effect of the project was that private commercial banks began to show interest during 1970 in long term development loans for small industry. Foreign banks in the country came under pressure to invest more of their funds in this sector rather than limiting their loans to short term credit to established businesses. The government of Nigeria was sufficiently encouraged by the results of the Centers to include them in the Second National Development Plan as part of its national policy for small industry development.

During the 1960s, the private sector became an integral component of USAID policy. By 1980, AID had supported over 1,000 projects which involved reinforcing the private enterprise sector in 75 countries. Because of their more attractive economic environment, Asia and Latin America were the largest recipients of such assistance. Owing to its perceived lower potential for private enterprise development, Africa received the least assistance in this sector. Following upon the projects in Brazil and Nigeria described above, there were small industry projects in the 1960s implemented in the Philippines, Taiwan, India, South Korea, Nicaragua, and Ecuador. During this period technical industrial advisors provided by the U.S. were assigned to government promotional or financial institutions. Most of them catered very little to small-scale enterprises. They were concentrated in medium and large scale industries in urban areas. To the extent USAID missions assisted small businesses, it was through private voluntary organizations and Peace Corps Volunteers. It is therefore accurate to observe that there was an implicit bias in favor of large-scale, capital intensive industry. There was a lack of appreciation for the actual and potential role of the small business sector and certainly inadequate knowledge of how the sector worked.

Issues in Development Assistance Policy

The New Directions Mandate, embodied in legislation beginning in 1973, shifted the emphasis in foreign assistance to basic human needs and the poorest of the poor. Resources for private enterprise development as it was conceived in the 1960s were significiantly reduced. A survey of USAID projects with a private enterprise component in the Africa region from 1950 to 1981, for example, showed that out of the total of $136 million worth of projects less than one-quarter were obligated after the New Directions legislation was enacted. During the 1970s there was a focus on rural development and a substantial expansion in support for socio-economic research on farms, eventually including rural enterprises as well.

The rationale for the New Directions legislation was rooted in disillusionment with reliance upon economic growth as the basic element of development strategy. Growth alone, it was argued by supporters of the legislation, did not reduce the incidence of poverty in developing countries. Supporters of the industrialization approach to development argued that the benefits of economic growth would "trickle down" to the poor. The critics of this approach which had prevailed during the 1960s pointed to examples of numerous countries where the benefits of growth were not reaching the poor majority. Donor funding, both bilateral and mutilateral, was shifted accordingly toward direct approaches to meet the basic needs of the poor. The private sector, with the exception of agriculture and, to a lesser extent, small scale rural enterprise, tended not to be a main component of the new programs. Development assistance moved away from a concern with industrialization as the main road to development toward local programs with a strong public sector orientation.

Under the Reagan administration the development model of the 1970s came to be seriously questioned. The tone for this line of thought was set by President Reagan at the summit meeting in Cancun, Mexico, in 1981. In essence, Reagan told the developing countries represented there that they should rely on their own individual initiative, stimulate private enterprise at home, and rely less on foreign development assistance. The critique of the prevailing approach to development assistance received amplification in an article by the Assistant Secretary of State for African Affairs, Chester Crocker, in 1981:

All too often...foreign aid in the last decade has created elaborate pilot projects which foreign countries can barely keep in operation, much less replicate. The maintenance costs of complex service-oriented projects, and, indeed, of much of the basic infrastructure that was created, in the absence of economic growth, have become unmanageable........ Without throwing out all we have learned about the basic human needs of food, health and education, nor abandoning all the programs we have now underway to build up African institutions, we must look afresh at the way our aid reaches or does not reach the productive sectors and how we can link social and humanitarian concerns once again with sound growth policies.

Numerous studies were commissioned to explore ideas and opportunities for private sector development initiatives. Discussion papers began to focus once again on the idea of the market place as central to an understanding of economic growth. Adam Smith was evoked as the point of departure for grasping the priority to be assigned to the free market as the engine of growth. Questions regarding development assistance became closely linked to those concerning the role of the United States in the world market place. How could U.S. business compete more effectively in the markets of developing countries? American perceptions of the importance of the Third World were changing. How could trade with these countries help the recovery of our own economy?

The recession forced the U.S. private sector and government agencies to explore new strategies for expansion beyond traditional markets for increased global competition. It was recognized that the ability of U.S. firms to function in developing countries could have a direct impact on the U.S. balance of payments, the employment situation, and industrial production. By January 1985 the flood of imports drawn into the United States by the strong dollar completely overwhelmed the best export performance in more than three years. The Commerce Department reported a trade deficit of $10.3 billion. In 1984 the United States doubled its trade deficit to a record $123.3 billion. A continued strong dollar led to predictions of increasing trade deficits. The largest deficit once again was with Japan, a total of $36.8 billion in 1984.

Indeed, Japan became the favorite whipping boy of the proponents of a more aggressive role of the United States in international trade. The Japanese were viewed as grossly violating the rules of free trade. They had launched successful marketing strategies in developing countries throughout the world, in spite of their differences in culture and language, geographical remoteness, and lack of historical association with most of them. But the Japanese devised a long-term strategy of market penetration rather than short-term profits. This strategy was buttressed by exchange control mechanisms, monetary and fiscal policies, and private investment insurance.

In francophone Africa, the French presence represented the greatest competition by far to U.S. investors. Here language and culture gave the French a tremendous advantage. But official government attitudes toward international commerical activities contributed a great deal to the French commercial success in Africa. Overseas trade and investment are considered to be of direct national interest to France. The French see trade with developing countries as being in their own domestic interest. Their own export-dependent industries benefit and jobs are created.

In each case the question of financial packaging seemed to feature prominently in the difficulties facing U.S. businesses competing in the same markets. Competitors provided mixed financing and liberal supplier credits, combined with unrestricted transfers of currency and simpler banking procedures.

Spokesmen for the U.S. private sector initiative declared these practices to be "predatory." The United States, they said, should fight fire with fire. The best way to move the world back in the direction of free trade would be to make these predatory measures too expensive for U.S. competitors.

Pauline Baker wrote a paper on the obstacles to private sector development in Africa and the possible U.S. policy initiatives. She concluded that despite the factors working against progress on the continent there were reasons to be optimistic. Baker saw the political climate in Africa changing, with a notable decline in the "orthodoxy with which ideological principles are promoted." She argued that the single greatest shortcoming of the U.S. private sector was in competitive financing. U.S. policy was to campaign for the elimination or reduction of subsidized export financing practices worldwide. But export finance and mixed credits remain critical factors in the capital scarce economies of Africa. She contended that U.S. firms were greatly disadvantaged by not being able to match favorable financing packages backed by other governments. Baker urged a number of other initiatives, including the promotion of increased commercial relations, as part of a program to make U.S. firms more competitive in African markets.

Elaboration of AID's Private Enterprise Policy

In 1982 the Agency for International Development produced its first policy paper on private enterprise development. The paper was based on the premise that greater reliance on private enterprise in Third World development is essential to the achievement of AID's central objective: to assist developing countries in meeting the basic human needs of their poor majorities. It was argued that much of the poor performance of low income countries could be attributed to policies that have inhibited market incentives. The most severe constraints to private enterprise development, it stated, are host government policies. The paper maintained that AID had not adequately pursued implementation of the portion of the legislative mandate which urged that the private sector be used to the maximum extent possible in development programs. It directed a "refocusing on the importance of free enterprise and the market mechanism in the development process."

The paper defined private as consisting of profit-oriented economic units producing goods and services for the market in which the means of production are privately owned. It specifically excluded private and voluntary organizations (PVOs) that produce marketed products, non-profit oriented or publicly-owned cooperatives, and parastatals (primarily government owned corporations). In a footnote it was pointed out that it is AID policy to support the strengthening of indigenous, development oriented PVOs and cooperatives. These organizations, together with private enterprises and private universities, constitute the private sector. While the paper noted that AID had not recently focussed on the industrial sector, it stated that support for small and medium scale enterprises is fully consistent with AID's legislation. Still, the paper had little to say about the nature of these enterprises and how to reach them. It made no mention of the informal sector in developing countries.

By 1983 there was a clear recognition by the Administration that the change of focus to private sector development should be written into legislative language. In May of that year the President established a Task Force on International Private Enterprise to examine how U.S. foreign assistance could be used to promote investment in and trade with developing countries. Most of the 21 members of the Task Force were chosen from the business community, from both large and medium sized firms.

In December 1984 the Task Force published its findings and recommendations in a two volume set. The report's basic conclusion: that the central policy that should inspire U.S. development efforts is its own experience. The way to create wealth, it stated, is to create incentives and to rely on the market mechanism rather than on government. The corollary to this axiom is that if developing countries do not accept this premise, development aid will fail.

The Task Force reviewed the history of U.S. foreign assistance programs. It concluded that not enough was being done to encourage or assist recipient countries in making the policy changes necessary to allow private sector growth. This was largely the responsibility of Congress for not having provided a clear direction either for the goals of aid or for the terms under which it should be provided. It was pointed out that the tendency over the past 10 to 15 years has been to put virtually all foreign assistance on a government-to-government basis. The Task Force lamented the fact that, in response to the New Directions Mandate and the basic human needs "doctrine", U.S. foreign assistance programs have emphasized meeting the needs of the poor rather than stimulating private sector growth. Public sector funds, it maintained, could only supplement resources that came from the private sector in the form of trade and investment.

The Task Force expressed a firm belief that primary emphasis must be placed on the long term, and that sustained economic growth depends on the private sector. Without rising levels of economic activity, basic human needs cannot be met. In attempting to convince governments of developing countries of the rightness of this point of view, the Task Force suggested that our own record of development gives the United States a credential that we should use far more boldly.

Turning its attention to the principal instrument of U.S. development assistance policy, the Task Force concluded that the scope of AID's private enterprise activities was too limited. In order to expand it, AID would need a clearer mandate, improved skills, and greater flexibility. Since 1981, this approach has been superimposed on the existing basic human needs approach. Although a Bureau for Private Enterprise was created to spearhead the effort, it was given a quite limited budget and staff.

These findings led to the recommendation that AID's mandate should be revised in legislative language, as well as its resource availability and organizational structure, to reflect a greater private enterprise emphasis. The Task Force suggested that Congress and the executive branch must recognize that private enterprise is synonymous with risk-taking. AID should therefore seek to engage private entrepreneurs in its development work by sharing risks itself. In the same vain, the Task Force recommended that AID serve more as a broker between U.S. businesses and prospective overseas partners by providing information on the investment climate and conditions in developing countries.

The Task Force report takes dead aim at the Congress in its insistence on the need for legislative change. Perhaps this will be seen eventually as the opening salvo in a public debate over the soul of development assistance policy. If this is so, the report merits careful scrutiny, not only for its basic premises but for its recipes for development programming. The report acknowledges the increasing economic interdependence between the United States and the Third World as the starting point. The United States is called upon to lead the world to a new era of prosperity by "unleashing the dynamism of the private sector in the Third World." But the report is equally concerned with the promotion of the security of the United States through the sharing of economic strength with the developing world. Indeed, the tone of the Task Force report is not in the least bit hesitant about touting the national interest aspect of development assistance as compared with its humanitarian motives.

The report is up-front in its analysis of the need to expand U.S. international trade. American firms are increasingly finding themselves competing overseas with foreign firms that are supported by their national treasuries. They are losing large amounts of business to (unnamed) "mercantilist" nations that provide heavy subsidies to their firms. This practice distorts the pattern of international trade to the detriment of both the United States and developing countries. The U.S. trade deficit increased sharply from $61 billion in 1983 to an estimated $130 billion in 1984. The Task Force proposes to face this problem head on with an aggressive program of counter-measures, including mixed credits financing. If other nations were not grossly violating the rules of free trade, it contends, there would be no need for these coercive and competitive measures.

The Task Force report implicitly acknowledges that the main instrument of this U.S. initiative should be large multinationals. The second volume Guidebook in fact devotes considerable attention to what it calls the IPEs (international private enterprises). It observes that small and medium-sized U.S. firms have engaged only modestly in overseas investment. The Guidebook further concedes that direct foreign private investment of the IPEs in the form of wholly owned ventures has caused resentment in developing countries. It then painstakingly refutes the "common prejudices" in developing countries against the IPEs. A few examples of these "prejudices" and the response to them suffice to illustrate this concern:

● Prejudice #1. It is often charged that the IPEs do not owe their allegiance to the countries in which they operate. Their main interest is the global transaction of production and sale rather than the development goals of the host country. Response: The developing countries should recognize that the IPEs can take risks that domestic enterprises cannot or will not take to develop new products and services. Their global distribution of resources and marketing have much greater potential for improved products and services.

● Prejudice #2. The IPEs are large economic units that can exert enormous power over local markets, giving them monopolistic positions that inhibit local business development. Response: If unduly constrained by host government policies, foreign firms are less likely to invest in local business development and market expansion.

● Prejudice #3. The business practices of large companies are abusive. Direct government intervention is the only way to force IPEs to make positive contributions. Response: Government interventions add costs and uncertainty to investment and commerical negotiation. When interventions are substantial, there is little likelihood that small and medium-sized foreign investors will attempt to enter the market.

The Guidebook concludes that developing countries are overcoming their reservations about large corporations. Experiments with foreign investment control in the 1970s have been at least partly abandoned in favor of inducements for foreign investment. This is offered as evidence that developing countries are coming around to the point of view that foreign investors should receive equal treatment to domestic investors.

From this review of the Presidential Task Force Report it is clear that at least some of the commission members were strong advocates of promoting an expanded role of the IPEs in development assistance programs. It must be assumed that this line of thought is well received at high levels within the administration, although it may not be part of the officially defined private enterprise policy. From this analysis of small business and development in preceeding chapters, however, it should be concluded that a development assistance strategy based on increasing the role of the IPEs is entirely misplaced. The alledged "prejudices" aginst the IPEs in the developing world can not easily be swept under the rug. A development assistance agenda aimed at promoting trade among U.S. small and medium scale businesses and those in developing countries is much more attuned to the development needs of the recipient nations. Even granting the economic growth emphasis on development, it is clear that small businesses represent the more dynamic sector of the U.S. economy and carry great potential in developing countries as the engine of development.

By 1985, AID's private enterprise policy paper had undergone substantial revision. Drawing upon the research conducted for the Presidential Task Force, a new policy paper superceded the previous one. The premise remained essentially the same: that a private enterprise economy is the most efficient means of achieving broad-based economic development. Government intervention in the market is seen as a hindrance to obtaining these objectives. "Except for small scale activities often characterized as informal, the economies of many developing countries are marked by extensive government efforts to determine production levels, prices, and consumption patterns." It is asserted that wherever the role of the public sector has been over-extended and the operation of the private sector restricted, developing countries have experienced slow growth, heavy budget deficits and rising debt burdens.

The revised policy paper offers rather more analysis and prescriptions for the "indigenous private sector" in developing countries than before. Without attempting to define the nature and extent of the private sector, the paper implicitly acknowledges the importance of the informal sector. Citing recent efforts to measure the extent of private sector activity in the Sudan and Peru, it suggests that "private enterprise is thriving" despite claims to the contrary. Peru's "underground economy" was found to absorb fully 60 percent of the work force. A large portion of the paper is dedicated to a discussion of the constraints to development due to government policies.

The first category of constraints concerns the government's strategy for economic development. Those countries that have elaborated a strategy of export oriented growth are seen as success stories. Those with a strategy of general import substitution, however, have been reluctant to expose their domestic markets to imports. They have not been receptive to policy changes which stress comparative advantages in products other than food grains while satisfying food requirements more cheaply through international trade. AID policy is therefore to encourage a shift from policies which promote general import substitution to those which open an economy to international trade. AID's strategy is to promote, through the policy dialogue process, a greater reliance on market determined prices and the initiative of the private sector.

A second set of constraints are government policies and regulations derived from the development strategy. These include the following:

• <u>Foreign exchange policies and regulations.</u> Most developing countries do not operate an open market in foreign exchange. As a result their foreign exchange rate often differs from that which would occur under free market conditions. The domestic private sector serving the domestic market thus usually operates in the black market, while foreign investors conduct their foreign exchange transactions offshore.

• <u>Import and export restrictions.</u> Many developing countries restrict certain types of imports and exports and severely tax some goods. Businesses are required to obtain licences prior to importing needed commodities. The issuance or denial of these licences is the mechanism by which the government substitutes political control for the economic judgments of the market place.

• <u>Market entry restrictions.</u> Often governments establish a complicated structure of rules and procedures related to the issuance of business licenses and the establishment of new businesses. Each step of the licensing process may require unoffical payments by the entrepreneur to move to the next step. In any case, long planning times impose a substantial cost which small-scale entrepreneurs lack the capital reserves to manage.

• <u>Limitations of investment.</u> Governments often specify a level of investment which they feel is warranted in a particular industry. Sometimes the specification is in the form of a limitation on the maximum size of private sector investment. This restriction is usually made to protect a large firm which may be owned by the government and would not be able to compete with a private firm of equal size.

● <u>Price-fixing</u>. Governments set a maximum price to maintain artificially low prices for certain goods. This is easiest to enforce when the government operates a price-setting parastatal. The most common items for price regulation are essential foods and agricultural inputs.

● <u>Taxation and use charges</u>. Governments tend to prefer in- direct taxes (on imports and exports) which are relatively more easy to administer than are direct taxes such as income or con- sumption taxes. This primarily effects the producers of export commodities, especially rural producers, and retards export growth. User charges, particularly for water, sewers, power and transportation rarely cover costs. The supply of these services must be financed in part from tax revenues.

A third category of constraints are policies that discourage private sector participation in traditional government programs. This applies to the social sectors such as health, agriculture and education. Government resources often cannot support the provision of services for all individuals who want them. But government policies and programs have restricted the operation of markets and entrepreneurs in these sectors.

The fourth category of constraints has to do with government ownership of enterprises and the designation of monopoly responsibility. It is common for developing countries to operate public enterprises without having to account for the real costs of operation. Revenues are rarely matched against expenses in terms of full cost recovery. The frequently poor record of state owned enterprises has become a drain on scarce resources and a liability to economic growth.

AID policy prescriptions to meet these constraints center on a strategy of policy dialogue aimed at encouraging the host government to undertake policy reforms. The intent of AID's private enterprise policy is to promote the establishment of a climate conducive to private sector activity in the host country. This means policies designed to build up the indigenous private sector rather than continued reliance on parastatals.

The remainder of the revised policy paper is devoted to specific components of AID policy. The paper is careful to iden- tify the Agency's target group as set forth in the Foreign Assis- tance Act (Section 101 and 102). It states that one of the four principal goals of foreign economic assistance is "...the alle- viation of the worst physical manifestation of poverty among the world's poor majority..." This is the crux of the New Directions Mandate. Reference to this objective was noticeably missing from the first policy paper of 1982, even though there were numerous quotes from the Act emphasizing private sector development. The revised policy paper further states that projects which implement

AID's private enterprise policy should clearly demonstrate the linkages between the activity which is to occur and the progress toward this primary objective.

The section on policy dialogue acknowledges the importance of the informal sector, heretofore essentially unnoticed:

AID believes that the operation of the heterogeneous, dynamic and largely unregulated informal economy pro-vides a powerful argument in favor of eliminating un-economic controls on the formal economy. In countries amenable to policy dialogue..direct AID assistance to enhance the importance of the informal economy is a valuable complementary program to policy dialogue with the (host) government.

This carries signficant implications for assistance to small scale enterprises in the informal sector. It recognizes that assistance to this sector may be the most effective way to reach AID's mandated target group. The sector includes large numbers of labor-intensive, capital-saving enterprises.

A Critique of the Doctrine of Economic Growth

Apologists for the private enterprise approach to development are given to arguing that those governments in developing countries that have played a predominant role in the economy have typically experienced real per capita growth averaging 3 percent a year over the past ten years. Some have been near zero growth. However, they say, those governments that have more narrowly defined the role of the public sector and allowed competitive markets to determine prices have experienced growth rates averaging 7 percent per year.

It is my contention that those countries that have followed a private sector development strategy while neglecting their small and medium sized enterprises are experiencing growth with-out development, or at best uneven development. A policy of development assistance that does not take this sector into ac-count is likely to fail, as it is charged the public sector ori-ented programs have failed.

● The Ivory Coast: Economic "Miracle"?

Students of African development have for several decades attempted to predict which countries were most likely to "take off" into sustained growth. In the 1960s it was believed that the minerals producing nations had the best chance for growth, with the potential to reach or surpass the seven percent gross natio-nal product (GNP) rate. Those that depended upon agricultural

90

products were given less chance of taking off. Some agricultural producers, such as the Ivory Coast and Kenya, were thought to be capable of succeeding, with proper management.

A 1981 World Bank report identified a group of countries which had achieved high growth rates over the past two decades: Botswana, the Ivory Coast, Kenya, Malawi, Mauritius, and Swaziland. All of them rely principally on agricultural products for export markets. But since the late 1970s even these countries have run into economic problems. Is this the reward for following the prescriptions for private sector development? What went wrong?

The Ivory Coast has long been cited as a paragon of progress, a "miracle of development." With a population of only 8.9 million in 1982 and a per capita income of $950, the country enjoyed one of the highest rates of production among the middle-income oil importers during the period since independence in 1960. The Ivory Coast was one of the few countries that managed to attain the seven percent rate of growth predicted for the minerals producing states, although its wealth was primarily in agricultural products. But by the beginning of the 1980s the Ivorian economy began to turn sour. In 1983 its external public debt was among the highest in Africa, estimated at $7.3 billion. Only Nigeria's debt (at $17 billion) was higher. By comparison, the external debt of Zaire stood at $4 billion, Kenya's at $3.1 billion, and that of Zimbabwe at $1.4 billion.

The Ivorian bubble started to burst in 1980. The commodity prices for the main exports of cocoa and coffee began to shrink. The substantial loans that had been used to fuel development of transportation and communication came due. The economy registered a negative growth rate in GDP during 1981 and 1982. There was a 50 percent deterioration in the country's terms of trade between 1978 and 1982 because of the reduced profits from cocoa and coffee exports. Inflation continued at a 10 percent rate, after an annual rate of over 12 percent during the 1970s.

Just as other African governments had been forced to bite the bullet of structural adjustment imposed by the International Monetary Fund, the Ivorians were faced with the necessity of reducing government expenditures. For example, the public investment program which had been the motor of development during the 1970s was sharply reduced. Agriculture continued to be the basis of the Ivorian economy, accounting for 90 percent of export earnings. Production was severely hampered by drought beginning in 1983. Coffee production for that year was half the normal yearly average. Meanwhile, the government was forced to import rice, wheat, and meat to satisfy consumer demands.

91

Since independence the Ivory Coast has maintained one of the most market-oriented economies in Africa, and even the entire Third World. But the commercial and industrial sector has been dominated by foreigners. In a candid speech delivered to the National Council in November 1983, President Houphouet-Boigny acknowledged this fact while deploring it. The speech was replete with references to free enterprise values and the need to "privatize" the economy even further. Ivorian commerce, he said, is in the hands of non-nationals: Asians, Europeans, and other Africans. One could "count on the fingers of one hand today the number of Ivorian commercant who have been successful." The President provided his own sociological analysis of the problem: Ivorians do not know how to save. They are inclined to spend large sums on such events as marriages and funerals. In his speech the President made reference to small and medium scale enterprises and government policy. He noted that because Ivorians as yet controlled no large industries, it would be necessary to develop small and medium scale industries first.

According to a 1980 census of industries in the Ivory Coast, there were some 15,000 small and medium scale enterprises, representing just over half of all firms and employing 25,000 workers. However, they accounted for only three percent of the value added in the modern sector. After over two decades of independence, more than 80 percent of all small businesses such as bakeries, butcheries, boutiques, bars, clothing stores, and service stations remained in the hands of foreigners. The few Ivorians who had succeeded were to be found in such industries as cosmetics and plastics.

The rapid growth of industrial output and value added in the 1960s and 1970s was based mainly on an import substitution strategy. As this approach began to face difficulties, emphasis was placed on large and medium scale export-oriented industries based on the processing of local raw materials. However, this was not accompanied by the expansion of small local enterprises, The predominantly foreign controlled large enterprises showed a preference for imports. While employment in the modern industrial sector doubled during the period from 1968 to 1978, employment within the small business sector stagnated for several reasons. Among these were government policies that favor modern, capital-intensive enterprises enjoying duty exemptions on the import of industrial goods. Furthermore, small businesses usually lacked access to credit facilities.

From a national development perspective, the strategy of industrialization followed during the first two decades of independence in the Ivory Coast raises serious questions. In the modern sector the distribution of wages and salaries between nationality groups has become increasingly polarized. Expatriates have been the main beneficiaries - and to a lesser extent Ivorian

workers - while non-Ivorian immigrant workers have faired poorly.
The strategy is not oriented toward the basic human needs of the
Ivorian society. Incomes of industrial salary and wage earners -
of whom expatriates and high income Ivorians represent a disproportionate share - have failed to induce consumption expenditure, and hence incomes of lower-income workers. Instead, they
have gone to imported luxury items and savings, much of it out of
the country. (It was reported that in 1980 profits and salaries
repatriated to France from the Ivory Coast were greater than
official French aid to the former colony.) Furthermore, industrial output has not been oriented toward the satisfaction of
basic needs as reflected in the food and construction industries.

Even though the modern industrial sector was for a long time
one of the most dynamic sectors in the economy, it has not fared
well in recent years. During 1981 and 1982, as overall growth
slowed, markets contracted. Although no major industries went
under, many of the small and medium sized businesses failed.
Numerous firms reported sales off by 25 to 30 percent. The
construction industry lost more than half of its jobs from 1980
to 1983.

This picture of a country considered to be a model of the
private enterprise approach leaves much to be desired in terms of
development. There is now a belated recognition of the need for
a strategy for developing the small and medium enterprise sector.
An indsutrial policy aimed at the promotion of employment and the
satisfaction of basic needs would encourage the establishment of
enterprises processing local raw materials and employing labor
intensive production techniques. Such a policy would attempt to
integrate the functions of small businesses into the larger
industrial economy. It would thus generate more employment per
production unit of increased output than traditional policies
favoring import-substitution of industry.

An ILO study in 1982 suggested that one policy change that
would help bring this about is the reform of the present fiscal
system which provides exemptions to priority enterprises on import duties on intermediate inputs and capital equipment. Direct
income subsidies should also be considered for industries that
use local raw materials. A set of reforms aimed at enhancing the
development of small and medium enterprises is also clearly in
order. Although the Ivorian government has given some attention
to this matter in recent years, critics contend that there has
been more form than substance.

● Malawi: Another Model for Private Enterprise Development?

The small land-locked nation of Malawi in southeastern
Africa is another of those few countries on the continent to have

experienced a positive rate of growth in per capita agricultural
production during the past two decades. A World Bank survey of
31 countries listed Malawi's policy performance as the best in
the sample. It is the only country in Africa deemed by the IMF
to be suitable for an Extended Fund Facility. Just as the Ivory
Coast, the government of Malawi followed a strategy of free
enterprise development with strong reliance on foreign investors
from the time of independence in 1964.

However, economic performance in Malawi suffered a marked
deterioration during the 1978 to 1981 period, just as in the
Ivory Coast. Weakness in policies such as low producer prices to
small farmers became manifest. The government of President
Hastings Kamuzu Banda succumbed to a program of extravagant
public expenditure and private credit expansion. Problems in the
public enterprise sector became apparent as management responded
to government demands for increased investment. The results were
disastrous. Economic growth came to a halt and for the first
time Malawi was faced with the same harsh choices already confronting other Africa nations.

Unlike the Ivory Coast, where the U.S. Agency for International Development does not have a bilateral development assistance program, the USAID mission in Malawi has been actively
involved in policy dialogue with the government of Malawi. USAID/
Malawi began to sharpen the focus of its strategy of bolstering
the country's sagging private sector in 1983. One of the targets
of project activity was the small and medium business sector.
Like the Ivory Coast, Malawi had failed to develop a policy of
stimulating small and medium scale enterprises. Some of the USAID
projects were designed to address this need. By mid-1984 the
mission had begun implementation of four private sector-directed
activities. Modest efforts were initiated using a combination of
approaches, including business and technical advisory services
as well as credit to smallholders and small and medium sized
businesses in the rural areas. The mission viewed these projects
as experiments to determine which approaches would be most effective.

As in the case of the Ivory Coast, the economic crisis in
Malawi is in part a reflection of the political conditions in the
country. Both countries have presidents in their 80s who have
exercised autocratic and paternalistic control over their people
since independence. Both political systems are characterized by
oligarchic domination of a bureaucratic and economic elite tied
directly to the president. Power is highly centralized in the
hands of a select few who owe their allegiance to the president.
The question of the presidential succession hangs over both
countries like a dark cloud. Whatever "miracles" have been
wrought in economic growth have been bought at the expense of
of participatory political development, since both presidents

94

have been reluctant to delegate any measure of political authority. The economy is dominated by foreign interests and state owned enterprises whose directors are the political proteges of the president and of course the president himself. This is precisely the problem with economic growth theories which tend to minimize political development.

Toward a Small Business Development Assistance Policy

As may be seen from this review of AID policy elaboration and examination of the economic growth theory underlying it, development assistance policy is still in need of critical assessment. It remains to be seen whether the private sector initative can be fashioned to meet the mandate to reach the world's poor majority while stimulating economic growth. An appropriate policy would seek to encourage more involvement of small and medium sized U.S. companies in partnership with firms in developing countries. One method of achieving increased international trade is through facilitating cooperative business relationships with U.S. firms through joint ventures, licensing, and subcontracting. These relationships should be based on the mutual desire of the involved firms to improve their competitive position in the world market and the need of developing countries for transfers of technology and managerial expertise.

Other U.S. government agencies are also mandated to assist in this objective. One of these is the Overseas Private Investment Corporation (OPIC). The primary purpose of OPIC is to provide risk insurance to U.S. companies interested in investing overseas. Until very recently most of OPIC's clients have been larger U.S. firms already well established in foreign markets. Beginning in 1981, OPIC undertook a concerted effort to inform small businesses of the market potential for private investment abroad. From 1981 to 1984, a total of 181 projects assisted by OPIC involved small businesses or cooperatives, still a small proportion of its portfolio.

Another agency whose purpose is to promote international trade is the Trade and Development Program (TDP). Its purpose is to help stimulate trade between U.S. companies and firms in developing countries. It aims at promoting exports from those countries while expanding markets of U.S. companies. Its premise is that what is good for development should not be inconsistent with what is good for the expansion of mutual commercial relations between U.S. and indigenous private enterprises. Here again, TDP programs almost exclusively reach larger U.S. companies and medium to large scale enterprises in the Third World.

U.S. development assistance policy elaboration thus far has been long on the identification of obstacles to economic growth and short on the design of programs to facilitate small business development. One USAID mission in East Africa described in a cable to Washington the obstacles to growth after ten years of a controlled economy, followed by modest efforts by the government to liberalize it. Licensing procedures for starting new enterprises are long and costly. Long-term credit facilities for the private sector are next to non-existant. Foreign exchange is difficult to obtain through the nationalized banking system, making spare parts, raw materials, and capital equipment scarce. Restrictive employment regulations continue in force and there is a lack of infrastructure and efficient services to assist private firms. Management and business skills have not been encouraged in the private sector. Most parastatals are operating at 25 percent capacity or are shut down.

These obstacles often seem almost intractable. Governments frequently are reluctant to accept the reform agenda prescribed in the U.S. government's policy dialogue. Meanwhile, the poor majority in developing countries pursue their survival strategies in the informal economy, while governments come and go. However, it is now being acknowledged that the informal sector in developing countries may play a far more important role than has been recognized. It is likely that small enterprises in this sector account for a significant portion of total employment and production. During the last ten years there has been a growing interest in these enterprises and their potential contribution to economic development.

Despite a growing number of surveys of the informal sector, donor agencies such as AID are still groping for ways to implement cost-effective programs of assistance to the sector. In 1978 AID's Office of Urban Development initiated a new program known by its acronym, PISCES (Program for Investment in the Small Capital Enterprise Sector). It consisted of two phases and six pilot projects in urban areas of the developing world. The research findings from the first phase of PISCES helped to gain a clearer picture of the informal sector. The survey confirmed the notion that the sector is a major source of employment for the poor, sometimes accounting for over half of those employed in urban areas. This sector is growing faster than the formal sector and seems likely to continue to do so, especially in areas with high in-migration rates.

In his report on the findings of PISCES I, Michael Farbman of AID noted that precise definitions of the informal sector are difficult to formulate. They may vary from region to region and from city to city. Some generalizations regarding small enterprises in the sector, however:

● Ubiquity. Hawkers and vendors, repairmen, artisans and small manufacturers are found in all urban areas.

● Small-scale. This feature applies to the number of workers as well as the amount of fixed and working capital.

● Localized. Activities meet the needs of local final and intermediate consumers.

● Labor-intensive.

● Low-income. Although not everyone in the informal sector has low incomes, most do; these are usually lower than unskilled earnings in the formal sector.

● Low profit. There is little opportunity for autonomous capital formation.

● Highly competitive markets.

The survey also confirmed many of the constraints faced by small enterprises in the informal sector, many of them derived from adverse government policies:

● Complex licensing and registration requirements and official harrassment

● Lack of management capacity

● Inappropriate technology

● Poorly developed human capital resources

● Limited access to raw materials and imported capital

● Poorly developed and limited markets for goods

● Limited access to credit

The PISCES study was then used to design projects to alleviate these constraints. The second phase of the project was aimed at assisting both existing businesses and creating new ones. This often involved providing credit and in some cases basic bookkeeping and management training to very small micro enterprises. Farbman concluded that credit was easily the most important resource made available by small informal enterprise assistance programs. Owners of businesses desire credit more than any other services. And credit is always identified as a necessary ingredient in the creation of new individual or collectively managed enterprises. The typical loan under the PISCES project was initially $25 to $100. Some went as high as $1000 in Ecuador, while minimum loans in the Philippines were set at $125.

As a result of the PISCES survey, it became generally accepted within AID that many opportunities existed for donor assistance to the informal sector. But it posed a number of questions and problems. It was seen as a high-risk sector. Assistance to it would likely always involve some element of subsidization. It was assumed that this was not an area in which donors could move large quantities of money. The smaller project sizes would suggest higher unit costs of development and implementation. Even though its beneficiaries would usually include the poorest people who fall within the congressionally mandated "target group," these concerns would likely incur resistance from an AID bureaucracy accustomed to moving large amounts of project funds aimed at government institutions.

The second phase of PISCES consisted of experimental projects which provided AID with experience in lending and management assistance to enterprises in the informal sector. Conventional wisdom argued against such assistance. But the PVOs implementing the projects learned from the experience, as did AID. They found that it is difficult to integrate social and economic objectives, while maintaining a strong "social policy" control over the business side of the project. They also learned that it is necessary to determine the absorptive capacity for loans to individual clients and to set loan policies accordingly. And, they discovered they needed more information on group formation when lending to cooperatives.

This approach to small business development has yet to become the new paradigm for AID programming. Indeed, many of the proponents of the private enterprise initiative consider that efforts at this level are rather fruitless, that the informal sector is not, after all, even part of the real private sector. They prefer to leave this sector entirely to the private voluntary organizations who have the patience to deal with it.

Conclusion

The new vocabulary of bilateral and mutilateral donor agency programs of development assistance to the Third World turns increasingly on the notion of private enterprise development. Programs of structural adjustment are offered as a crash diet to slim down over-indulgent government spending. Policy dialogue between the U.S. government and developing countries consists largely in attempting to persuade the latter to accept policies intended to minimize the role of government and promote a free

market. Some Third World governments have already bitten the
bullet and embarked upon reforms along these lines.

Beyond the policy dialogue process, however, is the question
of how technical assistance and technology transfer can be
employed to stimulate the private sector. We have seen that the
U.S. government has for quite some time been involved in projects
in the sector, but representing only a small portion of the total
AID program. With the creation of a new Private Enterprise
Bureau and directives to all USAID missions to emphasize the
private sector in programming, it is likely that this sector will
be expanded.

Development assistance is becoming viewed by some as a
weapon of the United States in the international trade wars, more
than an instrument of development for Third World nations.   In
this chapter it has been argued that an appropriate development
assistance agenda should focus on small business, both in the
United States and in developing countries.   To encourage
expansion of the activities of large U.S. corporations overseas
is not to contribute to labor intensive industry at home.   To
promote exports of small and medium sized U.S. firms would,
however, help accomplish this domestic objective.

Above all, an effective development assistance agenda should
not lose sight of the primary objective, which is to stimulate
development.   Small scale industries in the informal sector provide a means of livelihood to entrepreneurs and employment to
large numbers in this target group. In the next chapter a few of
the myriad of activities that begin to hint at the soundness of a
small business agenda for development will be examined.

Chapter Four References

A.W. Clausen, "Promoting the Private Sector in Developing Countries: A Multilateral Approach," speech delivered by the World Bank President to the Institute of Directors, London, England, February 26, 1985.

George Hawbaker, "Developing Small Industries: A Case Study of AID Assistance to Nigeria, 1962-1971," Washington, D.C.: Agency for International Development, December 1972.

Chester Crocker, "The African Private Sector and U.S. Policy," Current Policy, Nos. 348, November 19, 1981, p. 1.

Pauline Baker, "Obstacles to Private Sector Activities in Africa," paper prepared for the Bureau of Intelligence and Research, Department of State, January 1983.

AID, Private Enterprise Development Policy Paper, (revised) March 1985.

Mark Wentling, "The Development of African Private Enterprise," discussion paper, Office of Regional Affairs, Africa Bureau, AID, October 1981.

Molly Hageboeck and Mary Beth Allen, "Private Sector: Ideas and Opportunities, A Review of Basic Concepts and Selected Experience," AID Program Evaluation Discussion Paper No. 14, Office of Evaluation, Bureau for Program and Policy Coordination, June 1982.

Michael Farbman, "Providing Assistance to Informal Sector Enterprises: The Neglected Side of Urban Development," paper prepared for the East-West Population Institute Workshop on Intermediate Cities, Honolulu, Hawaii, July 16-28, 1980.

Galen Hull, "Political Risk Analysis in Africa: The Role of the Private Sector in the Ivory Coast," paper presented at the African Studies Association meeting, October 26, 1984.

Torkel Alfthan, "Industrialization, Employment, and Basic Needs: The Case of the Ivory Coast," ILO: Basic Needs and Development Programme, July 1982.

Chapter Five

A Small Business Agenda

"U.S. participation in the world economy is no longer tangential
to our economic performance, but a question of survival."

- President's Commission on Industrial Competitiveness
  January 1985

"Today we suffer from an almost universal idolatry of giantism.
It is therefore necessary to insist on the virtues of smallness -
where this applies."

E.F. Schumacher
Small is Beautiful, 1973

     What would the world look like if a program of action
centered on the development of small-scale enterprises were
adopted around the globe? This book has reviewed the role of
small businesses in the United States and in developing countries and has examined some of the obstacles that they encounter.
It is becoming increasingly evident that small business as both a
political and economic agenda is capturing the imagination of
many throughout the world. It is not simply a matter of chanting
"small is beautiful, small is beautiful." Small business offers
practical solutions to very ordinary problems, not a panacea.

     For many developing countries, a strategy of small business
development suggests a third way between a state socialist system
and a free enterprise system dominated by foreign capitalists.
In the United States, small business is becoming the rallying cry
of a few politicians of various colorations, left and right, who
see it as an instrument for challenging established special interests in the name of the public interest. Chapter Five looks
at some of the efforts that are being made to solve problems,
which taken together may hint at a small business agenda.

Small Business Trends in the United States

It has already been observed that many of the trends in small business promotion in the United States are taking place at the state and local level. Under the "new federalism" of the 1980s, state and local governments have emerged as economic development leaders in several areas.

● State Incubator Strategies

Incubators are intended for new enterprises that demand modest space requirements. They are typically for an entrepreneur who may be the lone employee in the firm. Facilities are basic, emphasizing the elementary needs of the business person. Incubators usually attract service and light manufacturing firms. They often consist of common office space, conference rooms, and mail services. They offer easy leasing arrangements to relieve the fear of starting and closing a business, or allowing rapid expansion. Incubators are frequently a mix between new and established businesses, thereby providing for a more stable revenue from rent.

A growing number of states and municipalities are promoting the entrepreneurial process through the establishment of business incubators which support the early stage of development of new ventures. There are several reasons for this surge of interest in incubators. In the first place, there is an awareness that new and young enterprises play an important role in the job generation process. There is also an increasing recognition that "smokestack industries" no longer constitute an effective development strategy. Locally "hatched" enterprises, on the other hand, are more apt to stay in the area, thereby providing a source of long-term job opportunities. There is a growing sense that incubators will play an important role in helping to reduce the high failure rates of new enterprises and revitalize local economies. The following states have experimented with policies designed to promote incubators:

Michigan. The state's Business Incubation Act allows the Department of Commerce to designate up to 10 vacant or nearly vacant buildings as business incubation centers. A community board is responsible for identifying potential sites and tenants, advertising the concept, and demonstrating a financial commitment of at least 50 percent for the first three years. The board - composed of political, financial, business, educational and labor representatives - selects tenants on the basis of their ability to serve a market need and likelihood of being profitable and creating jobs.

Pennsylvania. The state's Ben Franklin Partnership invites proposals from "local sponsors" to establish and operate incubator facilities. The sponsors include municipalities, local development districts, private non-profit and for-profit organizations approved by the Partnership. The sponsor is responsible for demonstrating the need for an incubator and explaining how it is to be set up. Loans from the Partnership cannot exceed more than 50 percent of total project costs, or $650,000, whichever is less. Loans may be used only for the acquisition of existing buildings and land, the rehabilitation of facilities, and the purchase of equipment. Capitalization of the program resulted from the passing of a $190 million bond program. In 1985 Pennsylvania had 18 incubators in operation and feasibility studies for another 18 underway.

North Carolina. The North Carolina Technological Development Authority is responsible for selecting potential sites for incubator facilities. It evaluates such factors as the area unemployment rate, the need for industrial and economic diversification, and the interest of the locality in the facility. The Authority can make one-time grants up to $200,000, to establish incubator facilities. Local governments and interests must match in cash or real estate value any grant made by the Authority. The non-profit corporation is responsible for managing and maintaining the incubator facility, and for developing a mechanism for providing technical and entrepreneurial expertise to residents. The program was initially funded with a $600,000 appropriation.

Kansas. In Kansas, the Department of Economics is empowered to establish state incubator facilities and to determine site selections. The department may make one-time grants up to $50,000 to establish incubator facilities. Only non-profit corporations are eligible for receiving grants, which must be matched by either cash or real estate. The corporation is responsible for managing and maintaining the facility and developing a mechanism for providing services.

● Lessons Learned from Europe

The importance of small business and its role in job creation and innovation is being recognized in Europe as well as the United States. The western European nations are faced with the highest levels of unemployment since World War II. They have increasingly rallied around the concept of local initiatives in general, and specifically small business development as a strategy for creating jobs. A report conducted for the U.S. Small Business Administration describes approaches to small business incubators as being rooted in the belief that there is no lack of potential entrepreneurs.

One such example is a British-based firm, Job Creation
Limited (JCL). The company was started in 1980 by former senior
executives of British Steel Corporation (BSC), led by Paddy
Naylor. In the 1970s BSC began closing plants and laying off
140,000 workers. Under BSC's sponsorship, Naylor and his associates created a new subsidiary in order to minimize the impact
of the layoffs. Thus, the first incubators were set up in communities where steel manufacturing plants were being closed down.
In 1975, the subsidiary began identifying company properties that
could be converted for re-use by new entrepreneurs. The idea of
promoting small business was still novel at the time.

The first major property conversion was started in 1977 at
Clyde Ironworks near Glasgow. Within one year it housed 50
tenants employing 250 people. By 1982 it had 61 tenants (90
percent of capacity) and a total of 316 employees. Half of the
tenants represented new business ventures. Similar successes
were occurring in other steel closure areas.

Naylor and his associates sensed that this idea could be
successful on the open market. So they established their own
for-profit company (JCL) in 1980. JCL has applied some of the
same techniques used at BSC in setting up other incubators.
Naylor and his associates believe that success depends on finding
property that can be converted into small, flexible, self-regula-
ting units. They seek to stimulate entrepreneurial ideas, no
matter how crazy they might seem at first. JCL offers basic
common services such as security, mail handling, and word processing. It also gives appropriate levels of management and financial advice, since the prospective entrepreneur needs to achieve
independence by establishing skills and an effective network.

- Unemployment Compensation as Self-Employment Tool

In 1985, Congressmen Wyden (D-Oregon), Schumer (D-New York),
and Gephardt (D-Missouri) introduced the Self-Employment Opportunity Act (H.R. 1690). This act would enable five to ten states
to create experimental pilot programs through which recipients of
unemployment compensation could continue to receive their benefits to help start up their own businesses. The authorization
would expire after three years and would require an evaluation of
the programs to determine whether they warrant further implementation. The two European programs on which the bill is based are
Chomeurs Createurs, started in France in 1979, and The Enterprise
Allowance Scheme, started in Great Britain in 1982. During the
past five years more than 250,000 people have participated in the
two programs.

104

● Association for Small Business Advancement

Clearly, some small business people are not waiting around
for government initiatives to promote their interests. In 1982 a
group of small business owners from the Washington, D.C., area
formed the Association for Small Business Advancement. The purpose of ASBA is to provide its membership with a little clout in
their financial dealings with banks. Traditionally, small businesses have had difficulty securing loans at interest rates below
prime. In 1984, according to the Federal Reserve Board, interest
rates on loans of more than $1,000,000 averaged 1.67 percent
below prime rate, while interest rates on those of less than
$25,000 averaged three percent above prime.

Under the logo of "Prime Busters," the ASBA is seeking to
organize smaller businesses in order to get better interest
rates.   The venture started with 30 companies and had grown to
over 300 by early 1985, ranging in size from sales of $150,000 to
$16,000,000. ASBA is a non-profit organization, charging annual
tax deductible dues of $750.   Members agree to establish their
checking accounts at the same bank. For example, Maryland members use the National Bank of Maryland, and District members the
National Bank of Washington.   In return, the interest rates
offered them are much lower than if they approached banks indivi-
dually.

Banks have shown an interest in ASBA for several reasons.
In the first place, firms that participate in the ASBA program
have to be "bankable," with a decent credit history, to become
members.   Banks are able to maintain deposits in non-interest
bearing accounts that they would not otherwise have. They see
the program as a good marketing tool to capture the small business market.   And business owners often end up doing more of
their other banking - such as car loans and certificates of
deposit - at the same institution.   The banker can build rapport
with the member firm, learning about the business and obtaining a
good picture of the firm's financing needs. Most of the bank of-
ficers have authority of at least $100,000, which means no loan
committees.   Small business owners seldom get this kind of service. Some bankers are pleased enough with the program that they
consider it the wave of the future. They consider that the movement has the potential to reshape small business bank borrowing,
and perhaps spread to other forms of financing.

● Small Business and Export Promotion

In the late 1970s and early 1980s, Americans at all levels
of government and in the private sector began to realize that the
international trade position of the United States was deteriorat-
ing. There has existed for some time a wide range of federal

government programs in the Departments of Commerce, Agriculture, and State which help exporters identify and assess potential markets. But direct federal assistance for export programs is declining. Record trade deficits, however, may spur the Congress to new trade promotion action. Meanwhile, Governors and mayors have begun to seek to define the obstacles to local trade promotion. They have found in surveys of small businesses that they lacked information about market opportunities, that they had difficulties with government regulations, that expenses incurred in developing markets were inhibiting, and that they had difficulty obtaining financing.

Several initiatives have been undertaken at the state and local level. In 1981, the U.S. Conference of Mayors released a guidebook entitled "Exports and Economic Development," with the assistance of the Department of Commerce. The guidebook in turn ushered in several other association publications and activities. On the state level, export programs have taken hold to some degree in nearly every state. The programs are usually administered by the state's economic development office and they tend to include such activities as trade missions led by state officials, trade fairs, seminars, and workshops.

Some small businesses have been successfully involved in the international market place for a long time. Such is the case with LogEtronics, a Virginia-based firm specializing in aerial photographic technology. Founded in 1955, the firm now has equipment in over 90 countries in the world. In 1984, LogE merged with an advanced technology computer imaging company so that together they had about 800 employees and $60 million in annual sales. LogE President Gordon Johnson urges other small businesses to look toward the export market. He has written about the elements of success in his company's export strategy. The key to its export growth, he says, has been to focus on value rather than price. In U.S. daily newspapers, where reliability of equipment is all important, LogE has manufactured over 70 percent of all the photographic processing machines in use today. That fact has been an asset for the company's overseas marketing strategy.

Johnson lists several rules for exporters. The first lesson in global marketing is that foreign markets must be viewed as a long-term commitment. LogE built up its international markets and distribution system over a 20-year period while the dollar was strong. He contends that "hassle factors" - such as greater risk and front-end financial commitments, foreign exchange transactions, foreign languages and attitudes - can be dealt with. He cites the range of programs at the federal and local level which are available to assist small businesses. But the most important single word of advice which Johnson offers, based on experience, is the need to have a full-time senior executive in charge of international marketing. Survival and growth in today's world require a global presence. The global market offers increased revenues and income as well as job opportunities.

An Entrepreneurial Policy Agenda for the United States

One of the most articulate voices for an entrepreneurial policy in the United States since the late 1970s has been the Corporation for Enterprise Development (CfED) in Washington, D.C. CfED is committed to improving the equity and vitality of the economy by enhancing the income-generating capacity of new and young enterprises. As the U.S. link in the Local Employment Initiatives Project of the Organization for Economic Cooperation and Development, CfED is part of a 20-nation effort to facilitate the international exchange of information in this area. CfED's monthly review, The Entrepreneurial Economy, devoted an issue to entrepreneurial policy in 1984. The general theme of the proposed policy would be to make it less difficult to bring new people and products to the market place. It is predicated on the belief that both the vitality and the equity of the American economy depends on this. The statement argues that an effective entrepreneurial policy must include these characteristics:

● It must be carefully aimed at the barriers to entry and expansion faced by new, young, and growing enterprises. They need equity, not debt, and under the present system they cannot take advantage of business tax incentives.

● It must be indirect and systemic since it is impossible to cut individual deals with hundreds of thousands of fledgling entrepreneurs.

● If it is to be even a partial answer to unemployment, it must generate thousands of jobs on the state level and millions of jobs on the national level.

● It must be cheap and rely on either redirecting existing public expenditures or private capital flows.

● It must be market-sensitive, designed to engage the energies and initiatives of a large number of people and institutions, but without pretending markets are perfect.

● It must address the range of public policy from income-maintenance and social-service policies to employment and economic policies.

Underlying these guidelines is the admonition not to fall prey to the myths surrounding private and public agendas. Private is not always efficient and public is not always wasteful. Properly designed programs should be viewed, not as mere expenditures of tax-payers' dollars, but as investments in the future prosperity of the nation. An entrepreneurial policy assumes a genuine belief in the ingenuity of the people. The only way of assuring this is to make certain there is reasonable access to the necessary support and investments.

The Entreprenuerial Economy then turns to a presentation of an agenda that encourages changes in eight basic areas:

• Stimulating seed and equity investment in new and young firms, as well as long-term, fixed-rate debt to growing firms by altering the regulation and behavior of private financial institutions and developing new institutions to provide risk capital;

• Gearing training and education programs toward activities with strong built-in job creating strategies such as entrepreneurial training;

• Using economic adjustment programs to aid dislocated workers and communities, but also strategies to create jobs;

• Revising income maintenance policies so that they not only mitigate the pain of dependency, but also support and encourage training, work, and job creation;

• Increasing research and development investments oriented toward new business commercialization;

• Building up the managerial skills of public institutions, non-profits, cooperatives, and employee-owned firms;

• Developing community economies by building a network of activities, not just single projects;

• Improving job quality by pursuing pay equity claims, fostering employee ownership and developing portable umbrella benefit plans.

And what about the political prospects for such an agenda? The Entrepreneurial Economy is persuaded that if an entrepreneurial policy emerges as a major focus of economic policy, it will most likely be at the state level. In recent years numerous state governments have begun to experiment with various kinds of entrepreneurial policies. They have focused less on luring branch plants of large manufacturing firms into their borders, and more on cultivating their own indigenous businesses.

108

The problem is, however, that the legislative politics of entrepreneurial policy are much more difficult than the electoral politics. While starting or running one's own business has always been a popular thing to do in the United States, entrepreneurship has, almost by definition, no vested interest. It is rather a collection of the would-be entrepreneurs along with those who recognize the importance of entrepreneurial values. An effective legislative strategy will thus require mobilizing organizations and individuals unaccustomed to participating in the political process. This would include social service agencies and advocates, civil rights groups, and trade unions destined to lose membership unless they focus on organizing the growing ranks of new and small businesses.

U.S. Development Assistance: Innovative Approaches

The movement toward small business promotion in the United States should not be viewed in isolation from developments in the rest of the world. Indeed, the careful reader will have observed that this is the very theme of this book! While we attempt to learn from our own experiences, we should be learning from the experience of others as well. Hopefully, too, people in developing countries have something to learn from examining the role of the small business sector in the United States. Those familiar with the U.S. development assistance industry, both practitioners and scholars, are all too much aware of the frequent failures of multi-million dollar programs of assistance to Third World governments which have scarcely left a development impact. Some innovative approaches to official U.S. development assistance deserve to be examined as possible models for the future.

● Small Farmer Production: Zimbabwe

A large portion of AID's programs center on improving agricultural production. In much of Africa, production has suffered serious reversals in recent years. In one of the few exceptions to this trend, Zimbabwe has continued to maintain an environment conducive to agricultural growth. At independence in 1980, the government of Prime Minister Robert Mugabe inherited a set of policies and institutions favorable to agriculture which had resulted in a very productive commercial sector comprised mainly of whites and a considerably less productive small scale sector of African small farmers. Since then, efforts have been successfully made to maintain and expand the infrastructure serving the sector. Government programs to increase the access of smallholders to needed inputs, markets, and technology have been increased with very positive results. After two consecutive years of drought, in 1984 Zimbabwe earned more than $500 million from agricultural exports.

Under a five-year program agreement signed in 1982, AID is assisting the government of Zimbabwe in the implementation of these policies. A program sector grant of $45,000,000 approved, following upon AID's agricultural sector assessment. The sector assistance format was chosen because it provides greater development focus and a closer linkage to agricultural policy than the cash grant mechanisms which had previously characterized AID assistance. The positive results of this program thus far have led some AID officials to urge the replication of this approach as a means of promoting privately organized farmer groups.

The keys to this success are to be found in large part in government policies which include an efficient marketing system, reasonable prices, and one of the best research and extension services on the continent. At the time of independence, about 40 percent of the land was reserved for 5,000 commercial farmers (mostly white) and about 40 percent for 600,000 small scale (African) farmers. As a result of government policies favoring the commercial sector, it produced 75 percent of total agricultural output and over 90 percent of marketed production. The country was self sufficient in nearly all food crops and was an exporter of several other commodities such as beef and corn.

The policy changes instituted since 1980 have been quite pragmatic, aimed at maintaining commercial output while expanding smallholder ability and incentives to produce. Despite his personal commitment to socialist principles, Mugabe encouraged white farmers to retain their holdings and continue capitalist-style production. At the same time, he attempted to improve the holdings of small-scale African farmers. He provided access to credit, extension services, and research. New grain depots and distribution centers were provided for seeds, fertilizers, pesticides and tools, financed in part under the AID sector assistance program. Small farmer credit increased from under 5,000 loans in 1980 to over 70,000 in 1984. At the same time interest rates rose from 7.5 to 13 percent for both large and small scale borrowers. There has been a shift in the focus of agricultural extension toward small scale farmers and settlers on resettlement schemes. In order to boost agricultural exports, the government has devalued the Zimbabwean dollar downward in stages by 50 percent since 1980.

Government policies have had social and political consequences as well. Farmers were encouraged to organize themselves into village groups which have emerged as effective channels for the expression of grievances and political leverage. Their voice combined with that of the commercial farmers is now an influencial lobby in the political system. In general, however, black Zimbabwean farmers tend to agree that life is better than it was before independence.

• Stimulating Subcontracting Relationships: Bangladesh

The typical approach to small enterprise development assistance has been described in preceding chapters. It generally addresses a capital constraint in which potential beneficiaries are paying exploitative interest rates. It often relies on highly motivated group behavior to absorb costs not borne by formal financial institutions. It frequently aims at microenterprises rather than medium-sized firms. Jan van der Veen, of the USAID mission in Bangladesh, has argued that another approach might prove more successful: promoting subcontracting relationships. Under this model, assistance is provided to the small firms indirectly and marketing constaints are attacked first.

Van der Veen argues that successful examples of this type abound, but are not recognized as comprising a generic model. In India, the diamond cutting industry has emerged as the principal, foreign exchange earner through an extensive merchant-based subcontracting network extending north from Bombay into Gujarat State. The industry employs nearly 300,000 workers and accounts for 12 percent of the country's export earnings. Although it was virtually non-existent 15 years ago, its growth has been phenomenal. In Thailand, the large multinational firm Charoen Pokphand has stimulated contract farming operations for decentralized pig raising by small scale farmers. There are several other examples involving subcontracting in farm production such as poultry, tobacco, shrimp, and vegetables. In Bangladesh, the rapidly expanding garment export industry, itself organized under subcontractual arrangements with international marketing firms, has begun to subcontract domestically with smaller firms.

In a typical subcontracting relationship, the smaller firm is charged by the parent company with manufacturing part or all of a product. The "charge" referred to is embodied in a contract. A firm may be designated a subcontractor if 50 percent or more of the value of its production is devoted to contract production. The subcontracting relationship may become regular and semi-permanent. Van der Veen suggests that this type of arrangement may be especially appropriate in countries such as Bangladesh where there is a large labor surplus and a weak entrepreneurial tradition except in the commercial sector. There is also excessive reliance on administrative rather than market allocation mechanisms.

In this context the primary constraints to many small-scale enterprises are managerial. Few small business owners can successfully devote their efforts to tasks in marketing, purchasing, technology, finance, and production all at the same time. The subcontracting arrangement limits attention mainly to production and labor relations. Marketing is assured by the parent company,

111

which can also assist on technological matters and sometimes with working capital.

USAID/Bangladesh is designing a small pilot project to explore the potential of a subcontracting approach in the light engineering industry. It is to contain a discount facility in which a credit line with a bank is made available to the subcontractor. Technical assistance will be provided in part by the parent firm. AID will provide assistance to the parent firm for training and partial guarantees.

● Assisting Women Entrepreneurs

Women's income-generating projects in the Third World have frequently been characterized by their failure to achieve self-sufficiency, and by their continued dependence on implementing agencies. In fact, until recently few development projects at all attempted to tap the latent potential of women-owned businesses which constitute a significant portion of the Third World's micro enterprises in the commercial sector. In 1980, the Human Resources section of AID's Program and Policy Coordination branch awarded a grant to The Pathfinder Fund, a private voluntary organization, to carry out a three year action-research program in Latin America and the Caribbean. The program selected five women's group-owned productive enterprises operating in the informal sector. Grants, rather than loans, were provided for capital equipment, training, and initial production costs. The objective was to help them attain financial and managerial self-sufficiency by the end of the two to three year grant period.

The five projects funded were: a metalworking enterprise in Bahia, Brazil; an ice cream factory in Limon, Costa Rica; a poultry cooperative and a bakery in rural Honduras; and a crafts and sewing enterprise in rural Jamaica. Together, the projects benefited approximately 100 preliterate and semi-literate women. Most of them tended to rely on occasional and seasonal means of earning cash such as street vending, agricultural labor, sewing, and domestic labor. All five projects produced goods in quantity and quality to be sold in the formal market. Training and equipment were provided by a grant from The Pathfinder Fund. The working capital and salaries of the women were generated from their savings of income from the use of the equipment.

By December 1984, all of the projects were still operating. Three of them were generating enough income to meet current expenses and four had sufficient working capital for cost-efficient production. The principal obstacle to long-term profitability in all of the projects was marketing. Four of the enterprises had achieved a legal status making them eligible for credit, although it was too early to tell whether this would translate into access in reality. In its report on the impact of the projects, The Pathfinder Fund claimed that the projects had had "an enormous impact on the lives of the women and their families" and varying degrees of impact upon their communities. As individuals, many of the women experienced a dramatic increase in self-confidence and assertiveness. And they learned bookkeeping and managerial skills as well as technical productive skills.

The report summarized those factors identified as contributing to the success of the projects. Group ownership was seen as important in promoting the commitment of all members to the well-being of the enterprises, helping them to weather difficulties. In some cases commitment to the group was so strong that women continued working when there was no income. In those projects where marketing and feasiblity studies were conducted before funds were committed, performance was better. Local availability of technical assistance was found to be a critical factor in allowing the project to use more sophisticated technology. Securing legal status for the enterprise made them eligible for credit and the benefits of sectoral government programs. On-the-job training was provided by technicians in all aspects of group production, management, and marketing. A key element of this participatory and analytic training was practice in evaluation, decision-making, and group formation.

AID programming is moving slowly in the direction of efforts to assist small and medium-scale enterprises in a variety of ways. With the increased emphasis on participant training, there is renewed interest in bringing Third World entrepreneurs and business executives to the United States for short term management training and internships with U.S. companies. There are an increasing number of programs intended to provide technical assistance to develop the capabilities of institutions which assist small and medium-sized enterprises. However, these discrete project activities need to be complemented with creative solutions from outside of the traditional institutional channels. Some of the ideas being put forward would involve increased public development assistance in new forms, while others appeal to the enlightened self-interest of the U.S. private sector.

Development Assistance Proposals

● Wholesaling Capital for Micro-Enterprises

Frank Penna, an associate of the Policy Sciences Center in New York, has been promoting possible legislative initiatives to assist micro-enterprises (employing one to five persons) in the developing world. The Center's agenda calls for increased financial assistance to micro-enterprises through wholesalers of capital. Penna has suggested that assistance could be provided

113

through existing institutions such as USAID and development banks, by creating an international bank for micro-enterprise development. He has also suggested organizing a world conference on the financing of micro-enterprises.

Enterprises in the informal sector are usually family owned and operated, often in occupations such as tailoring, carpentry, and small-scale farming. They require relatively low capital investment, not only to create jobs but to increase income as well. But these enterprises are often desparately in need of capital and are forced to borrow at usurious rates of interest.

The retailers of capital to micro-enterprises consist of three types of financial organizations: for-profit firms that are unregulated (in the informal sector), for-profit firms that are regulated (in the formal sector), and non-profit organizations. Those in the informal sector include numerous types of moneylenders, ranging from family and friends to unscrupulous middle-men. Estimates are that 50 to 70 percent of the finance in the informal sector is through this channel. The second category includes indigenous commercial banks, which sometimes reach millions of borrowers. Those in the third category include indigenous development foundations such as the Solidarios in Latin America.

Wholesalers of capital fall into three general categories: indigenous central banks, bilateral government agencies, and multilateral agencies. Central banks, such as the Reserve Bank of India, have occasionally provided a source of capital and guarantees to retailers for micro-enterprise lending. Bilateral agencies such as USAID also provide capital to both for-profit and non-profit retailers. Multilateral agencies provide wholesale sources of capital as well. The International Fund for Agricultural Development (IFAD) is the only one with a window for ongoing lending to micro-enterprises. For example, IFAD capitalized the Grameen Bank in Bangladesh with $38 million.

The problem with wholesalers is that large loans tend to crowd out micro-enterprise loans. Large loans are always more economically attractive than smaller ones. The result is a small amount of capital allocated at the wholesale level. For example, even at the window of the Inter-American Development Bank there is less than $10 million available per year to small enterprises out of the Bank's total lending of $2 to $3 billion.

Penna has suggested exploring legislative initiatives in the following areas:

● USAID. The Congress could specify that a minimum percentage or amount of money be set aside for micro-enterprise lending. Legislation could also stipulate conditions for all

114

loans (for large and small enterprises) that would induce changes in government policies to facilitate lending at this level.

● Development banks. Congress could recommend the creation of windows for the development banks such as the one at the Inter-American Development Bank. The windows might be capitalized with one to ten percent of each bank's profits. In the case of the World Bank, this would mean an allocation of $10 million to $100 million.

● International Bank for Micro-Enterprise Development. Legislation could propose that USAID explore the feasibility of establishing a bank that would generate capital through shareholders and bond sales. Such a bank would then wholesale that capital to retailers in developing countries.

● International Poverty Bank

Another proposal which follows along similar lines has been floated by Jeffrey Ashe, senior associate director of ACCION International, a private voluntary organization headquartered in Boston. The idea of an international poverty bank grows out of ACCION's nearly 25 years of helping local organizations start micro-lending projects throughout the Americas. By 1985, the fourteen projects assisted by ACCION were lending to more than 8,000 micro-entrepreneurs.

ACCION has observed in its work with micro-enterprises that direct assistance efforts run by banks and other financial institutions often intimidate the would-be borrower. They present obstacles such as legal registration, property titles, and collateral requirements. They are expensive and time-consuming to the small entrepreneur, necessitating repeated visits and endless waiting at the bank. Oddly enough, the credit provided by banks is often ill-suited to the needs of business owners at this level because too much money is loaned for too long a period. Defaults and late payments often plague bank lending efforts.

The goal of the proposed international poverty bank would be to upgrade the smallest self-initiated economic activities of the poor and stimulate the creation of new small business ventures. Lending could also be conducted through a micro-enterprise window in existing donor institutions. This could be accomplished by encouraging local financial institutions to create special micro lending units, such as the Grameen Bank in Bangladesh. Local financial institutions could be encouraged to on-lend to the projects of local non-governmental organizations. The bank could begin by synthesizing the relevant experience in micro-lending to date and develop criteria for project selection. It could develop packages for establishing revolving loan funds, training local staff and business owners, and improving business management.

The rationale for the proposed bank is to overcome the traditional problems of most existing programs financed by donor agencies in loaning to smaller local organizations because of their own transaction costs. The international poverty bank would have to be "agile, responsive, and flexible" in order to be effective. Ashe suggests that parameters would have to be established for approving ongoing financial assistance. The first grant to a local project would be issued for a small amount. Minimum standards might include:

● Loan losses - less than five percent of value of the current loan portfolio;

● Average loan size - less than $25/month, $300/year;

● Women participants - better than half of the total;

● Interest rates - commercial or higher.

● Blocked Funds at the Service of Development Goals?

The realities of the international financial order may conspire to bring large U.S. corporations into the business of assisting small businesses in the developing countries. As noted in Chapter One, many companies operating in the Third World are unable to remit earnings from those countries to the United States in dollars because of local foreign exchange controls. The dollar exchange value of these earnings is being rapidly eroded by inflation and devaluation.

One of the solutions to this predicament can work to the advantage of both the corporation and the host country. Several larger U.S. firms are already contributing these blocked funds to private voluntary organizations (PVOs) which may receive tax-deductible contributions under U.S. law. The PVOs then use the funds for their programs within the country where they are contributed. The company recoups a substantial part of its blocked funds through a tax-deductible contribution. The PVOs reinvest the funds within the country by assisting such activities as food production, primary health care, and small business development.

This approach to the disposition of blocked funds may thus earn the approval and respect of the countries where the company has investments and markets. It encourages the company to reinvest in the productive capacities of those countries. And it may also contribute to the increased awareness of corporate executives of the development needs of other people.

Small Business and Productive Energy in the Third World

When all is said and done, the productive energies of developing countries will likely be unleashed by the people themselves regardless of the commitment of international donors and private firms, or the lack thereof. Therefore, one should perhaps pay closest attention to those enterprises which spring from the indignenous resourcefulness of the people. The most mundane of human needs, as well as age-old cultural traditions, give rise to entrepreneurial efforts. The following examples provide a random selection of such enterprises.

● The Easy Toilet Society: India

Mahatma Ghandi made "cottage industry" a household term in India and around the world several decades ago, when that country was newly independent. While Ghandi's program did not succeed in abolishing poverty, the legacy of his concern for poor people still lives. Some untouchables - or bhangis - manage an existence by going from house to house carrying away buckets of human excrement balanced on their heads. Ghandi waged a campaign to liberate these "night soil" scavengers from their demeaning labor. Today there are still some 650,000 bhangis collecting bucket privies and dumping them in fields and canals. This practice is a hazard not only to their own health but to that of their neighbors.

Recently, encouraged by the Indian government and the United Nations, several private voluntary organizations have been making inroads into the scavenger system,. They are installing low cost, flush latrines with underground septic tanks while rehabilitating thousands of bhangis in the process. One of the most successful of the voluntary scavenger emancipation enterprises is the Easy Toilet Society, which has started a modest revolution in sanitation planning by using entrepreneurial business practices and modern aggressive marketing methods. Begun in 1973 by Bindeshwar Pathak, the non-profit society hopes to persuade the government to undertake an anti-scavenger program similar to family planning, so as to eliminate the lowly occu- pation from the Indian caste system.

117

Mr. Pathak, a former civil servant frustrated with the bureaucracy, eschews government funding and has not recieved any grants. The society receives 15 percent of cost for supervising construction of sanitary facilities. It reinvests all of its profits back into expansion, research, and social rehabilitation programs. Easy Toilet now operates more than 300 public toilet facilities in seven states. Its biggest expansion has been in building low-cost flush latrines in private homes. More than 300,000 have been installed in ten years.

Ironically, some of the strongest resistance to the emancipation programs conducted by Easy Toilet and other societies has come from the scavengers themselves. Night soil scavengers working for municipal governments earn about $40 a month. Many of them are women, untrained for any other job, who view the "liberation" movement as a threat to their livelihod. The Easy Toilet Society has begun retraining programs to convert the scavengers into auto mechanics, drivers, taliors, and typists, as well as assembly-line workers in factories manufacturing ceramic flush toilets!

● Mondragon: Spain

Mondragon is one of the most impressive and well known experiments in worker-management in the world. Many consider it to be the prototype for participatory development, moving beyond the stage of rural cooperatives to a mixture of agricultural and industrial production. Mondragon was the creation of Don Jose Mario Arizmendi, who died in 1976. Arizmendi was a man of the cloth, but very much in the world. He combined elements of Spanish industrialization, Basque nationalism, and the labor movement to promote Mondragon, beginning in the 1950s.

During its initial stages Mondragon promoted the creation of cooperatives and a credit bank. The first co-op started in 1956 with 24 employees. By 1979 there was a federation of cooperatives with over 15,000 employees. One of the distinguishing features of Mondragon is its organizational structure, consisting of several levels of councils. The supervisory board is elected by the general assembly and is responsible to the co-op members. The Board appoints the managers of the co-op. This indirect accountability of management is considered to be one of Mondragon's strengths.

Today Mondragon is a major employer in the region. To agricultural, educational, housing, and service co-ops have been added retail co-ops. Resources were originally mobilized in the 1950s from the local community, against specific commitments to provide jobs for new workers. From the 1960s onward the co-op credit bank played the key role in financing programs. In a study of Mondragon by Henk and Thomas published in 1982, the organization's growth record was found to be quite impressive, compared with conventional companies. Mondragon registered a high rate of investment as a percentage of value added during the 1970s. There were high rates of profit, most of which was reinvested in the organization. Problems of credit have been kept to a minimum because of the recycling of profits.

In a review of 18 successful development projects, development specialist Guy Gran found Mondragon to be especially impressive because of its continuous learning process. The combination of study and work envisioned by Azimendi eventually became institutionalized. Today there is a co-op dedicated exclusively to research and development and an elaborate network of educational co-ops which meet planning and manpower needs. The Mondragon organization has served as inspiration for worker-management experiments elsewhere in the industrial countries as well as the developing world.

● The Al-Roadhah Weavers Cooperative: South Yemen

One of the legacies of the late E.F. Schumacher is the Intermediate Technology Development Group (ITDG) which he founded in Great Britain in 1965. Today ITDG carries on the tradition of gathering and disseminating information about the choice of technologies appropriate for small enterprises in developing countries. Among its most well known associates is Malcolm Harper, Professor of Enterprise Development at Cranfield School of Management. He and Kavil Ramachandran, a consultant to the Andhra Pradesh Indusrial and Technical Consultancy Organization of India, have edited a collection of 28 case studies from 17 countries that describe the problems and successes of small enterprises. They are drawn primarily from projects studied by the annual Cranfield program to promote small-scale enterprises, and from materials provided by the International Labor Office on industrial cooperatives.

The selection includes such activities as garment manufacturing, handcrafts, and vehicle repair, as well as more unusual ones such as sculpture, aluminum hollow-ware, and a steel-rolling mill. The authors note that some two thirds of the case studies describe what might be called failures. About half of them concern cooperatives, which receive a disproportionate amount of attention from local and international assistance agencies. Most of the cases are from Asia and Africa, with a few from the Caribbean region, the Middle East, and the South Pacific.

Al-Roadhah is a small town in the People's Democratic Republic of Yemen, located about 350 kilometres from the capital city of Aden. Since time immemorial Al-Roadhah has been a traditional center for weavers. The shawls made there are similar to those which were sold in the ancient markets of Mesopotamia, Persia, and the Mediterranean over 2,000 years ago. In recent years, modern mass-produced goods have come to dominate world markets. Many of the traditional Yemeni handcraft industries have disappeared because they could not compete with imported commodities. As a result, the skills of the craftsmen have tended to deteriorate.

Since independence in 1967, The Revolutionary Government of South Yemen has attempted to remedy this situation, by preserving and promoting these industries. In 1971, a special decree was issued to allow the leather handcraft workers of Aden to form a cooperative, and from then on the concept was spread to other industries around the country. One of these was a group of 44 men who formed the Al-Roadhah Weavers Cooperative in 1974. They had all been weavers for many years. They were interested in ensuring a regular and reasonably priced supply of raw materials, improving the marketing of their products and their working conditions. And they hoped to promote employment and preserve their craft by attracting young people to the trade.

At the beginning the members contributed a total of $300 share capital. The government arranged an interest-free overdraft for them at the National Bank of Yemen which enabled the group to finance its activities. Their first project was to obtain raw materials for weaving the traditional men's kilts which were the main item of production. They had a problem securing an adequate quantity and quality of materials, and the cooperative nearly folded. But then things took a turn for the better when they were able to obtain raw materials from Japan. They began to encourage women to join the group, forming a totally new production unit and using a modified hand-loom that improved production. Since then Al-Roadhah has been successful in expanding its operations, increasing wages of its employees, and re-investing its surplus in its own operations.

Harper and Ramachandran note that this is an unusual and encouraging example of a successful cooperative in a country which has a strong ideological commitment to state and community enterprise. In contrast to other similar ventures elsewhere, the government simply provided the legislative framework within which the craftsmen could begin cooperatives. It provided modest assistance in the form of an interest-free loan and training services but has not attempted in any way to take over the operations of the cooperative.

● The Retladira Welding Works: South Africa

This case study is notable for the insight it provides into the effect of the South African government's policies of apartheid on an African enterprise. M.J. Gomba was a skilled worker

120

employed in a factory which manufactured bodies for motor vehicles near Pretoria. In 1975 he decided to go into business for himself. He bought an arc-welder and started to make security bars to protect houses against burglars, initially on a part time basis.

Because South African law prohibits Africans from operating businesses except in the so-called "homelands" which are a long way from the major markets and sources of raw materials, Mr.Gomba had to operate in his backyard. There was, however, a great demand for his products. After three months he gave up his job at the vehicle company and hired three people to assist him in his business. Within four years he was doing so well he bought a new van in which he could deliver his products to the sites where they were to be installed. In order to expand, he realized that he would have to obtain proper premises, which would mean moving to his "tribal homeland" 30 kilometres away. He concluded that the advantages of a legal location would outweigh the advantages of continuing to work where he was.

Mr. Gomba then set out to obtain a license. After going through lengthy procedures he succeeded in establishing a legal business and building the Retladira Welding Works on the cite allocated to him by the traditional "homeland" chief. He invested his own savings of $56,000 in the building, retained three full-time workers, and paid himself a decent salary. Although his business has been successful, Mr. Gomba still has problems. In South Africa it is very difficult for Africans to sell to, or even buy from, large non-African businesses. Even if he can find a purchasing agent willing to deal with him, the social barriers make it hard to form any lasting business relationships. In any case, he faces very keen competition from larger non-African businesses which are able to buy material in greater quantities and manufacture their products on automatic machinery.

Mr. Gomba must rely largely on the African market, which also carries problems. Africans in South Africa have come to believe that products made by their own people are necessarily of a lower standard than those that come from large, internationally known companies. Those Africans who are relatively well off live in the townships outside the "homelands." The people living around his factory are generally very poor, and only a few of them commute to jobs in the townships. Most depend on subsistence farming for their livelihood and therefore offer a very modest market for Mr. Gomba's products. He would prefer to be able to relocate his factory in a township but only those African entrepreneurs with good connections can manage that.

Conclusion: Toward a Small Business Agenda

Small businesses throughout the world share common features and similar problems. New and young enterprises in particular are faced with difficulties in securing a license, obtaining credit, and acquiring facilities and equipment. Cultural and social traditions condition the entrepreneurial environment to a large extent. Theories about entrepreneurship are beginning to take account of these factors as well as the more obvious economic and political factors that have been used to explain its development. Public policies can be used to discourage small business development, but when designed properly can also help to promote it.

Some students of small business development argue that the proper role of government is simply not to intervene at all in the market place. In the United States, this point of view contends that the best policy is one of tax incentives to business. Others maintain that government programs can do more to stimulate the growth of new and younger enterprises. It has been argued in this book that an entrepreneurial policy should seek ways of making credit and technical assistance available to small businesses.

It is becoming clear that in the Third World, official programs alone cannot achieve a great deal unless the policy environment is favorable. Even then they can claim no more than a catalytic role. It is even more important, as Harper and Ramachandran point out, that the individual or groups with whom they are dealing should possess the necessary entrepreneurial qualities. Those of us who are interested in promoting these activitie can assist by intensifying the search for techniques to identify such people and take part in the public policy debates surrounding these issues.

Chapter Five References

Michael Greene, "Creating Jobs by Creating Employers: State Incubator Strategies," The Entrepreneurial Economy, April 1985.

Renée A. Berger, "The Small Business Incubator: Lessons Learned from Europe," paper prepared for the Office of Private Sector Initiatives, Small Business Administration, (no date).

"Small Businesses Prove Old Adage: In Numbers There is Strength," in Growth Capital: Newsletter of Entrepreneurial Finance, Vol 4, No. 2, January 1985.

Peter J. Levine, "Local Government Export Programs," in Export Today, Summer 1985, Volume I, No. 2.

Gordon O.F. Johnson, "LogEtronics, Inc.: Profile of An Evolving Export Strategy," Export Today, Summer 1985, Vol. I, No. 2.

Glenn Frankel, "Zimbabwe's Mix of Incentives for Peasant Farmers Raises Output at a Time of Famine," Washington Post, November 24, 1984.

Marc Winter, "Zimbabwe Agriculture," end of tour report circulated as memorandum within AID, February 4, 1985.

Jan van der Veen, "Stimulating Subcontracting Relationships: An Alternative Approach to Developing Small and Medium-Scale Enterprises," paper presented to AID Economists Conference at Annapolis, Maryland, November 1984.

Libbet Crandon, "Women, Enterprise, and Development," report prepared for the Pathfinder Fund of Chestnut Hill, Mass., Women and Development: Projects, Evaluation and Documentation Program; funded by AID, Bureau for Program and Policy Coordination, December 1984.

Frank Penna, "Wholesale Capital for Micro-Enterprises: Possible Legislative Initiatives," paper presented to the House Select Committee on Hunger, May 8, 1985.

Jeffrey Ashe, "An International Poverty Bank: Some Initial Thoughts," paper presented to the House Select Committee on Hunger, May 8, 1985.

William Claiborne, "Scavenger Class Still Does India's Dirtiest Job," Washington Post, May 13, 1985.

Guy Gran, "Learning from Development Success: Some Lessons from Contemporary Case Histories," prepared for NASPAA (National Association of Schools of Public Affairs and Administration and funded by AID, Bureau for Science and Technology), Working Paper No. 9, September 1983.

Malcolm Harper and Kavil Ramachandran, Small Business Promotion: Case Studies from Developing Countries, London: Intermediate Technology Publications, 1984.

Selected Bibliography

Books and Articles

Alfthan, Torkel (1982) "Industrialization, Employment, and Basic Needs: The Case of the Ivory Coast," ILO: Basic Needs and Development Programme, (July).

Baker, Pauline (1983) "Obstacles to Private Sector Activities in Africa," paper prepared for the Bureau of Intelligence and Research, Department of State, (January).

Bromley, Ray (1985) Planning for Small Enterprises in Third World Cities, New York: Pergamon Press.

Brown, Jason (1984) "Small-Scale Bank Lending in Developing Countries: A Comparative Analysis," paper prepared for AID, Office of Rural and Institutional Development, Bureau For Science and Technology, (April).

Brown, Raymond L. (1982) Indigenous Entrepreneurship in Less Developed Countries: The Importance of Entrepreneurs to the Development Process, Claremont Graduate School, unpublished dissertation.

Bruch, Mathias and Ulrich Hiemenz (1984) Small and Medium Scale Industries in the ASEAN Countries: Agents of Victims of Economic Development?, Boulder, Colo.: Westview Press.

Chuta, Enyinna and Carl Liedholm (1979) Rural Non-Farm Employment: A Review of the State of the Art, Michigan State University, Department of Agricultural Economics, Paper No. 4, Rural Development Series.

Clausen, A.W. (1985) "Promoting the Private Sector in Developing Countries: A Multilateral Approach," speech delivered by the World Bank President, February 26.

Coquery-Vidrovitch, Catherine (1983) Entreprises et Entrepreneurs en Afrique: XIXe et XXe Siecles (tome I), Paris: l'Harmattan, papers presented at a colloquium held under the auspices of l'Agence de Cooperation Culturelle et Technique.

Crandon, Libbet, et. al. (1984) "Women, Enterprise, and Development," report prepared for the Pathfinder Fund of Chestnut Hill, Mass., Women in Development: Projects, Evaluation, and Documentation Program, funded by AID, Bureau for Program and Policy Coordination, (December).

de Oliveira, Fransisco (1985) "A Critique of Dualist Reason: the Brazilian Economy Since 1930," in Bromley cited above.

Dickson, Paul (1985) "The New Entrepreneurs: The Urge Intensifies," in Creative Living (winter).

The Entrepreneurial Economy: The Monthly Review of Enterprise Development Strategies (editorial), "Reducing Unemployment Through Entrepreneurial Policy," January 1984.

Gran, Guy (1983) "Learning from Development Success: Some Lessons from Contemporary Case Histories," prepared for NASPAA (National Association of Schols of Public Affairs and Administration) and funded by AID, Bureau for Science and Technology, Working Paper No. 9, (September).

Harper, Malcolm and Kavil Ramachandran (1984) Small Business Promotion: Case Studies from Developing Countries, London: Intermediate Technology Publications.

Hertz, Leah (1982) In Search of a Small Business Definition: The U.S., the U.K., Israel, and the People's Republic of China, Washington, D.C.: University Press of America.

Hull, Galen (1984) "Political Risk Analysis in Africa: The Role of the Private Sector in the Ivory Coast," paper presented at the African Studies Association meeting, (October 26).

INC: The Magazine for Growing Companies. (April - June, 1985)

Jeune Afrique Economique, "Entreprises Africaines: 700 Leaders," special edition, December 1984.

Kilmer, Gary (1983) "The Policy Environment for Enterprise Development in Central Java," Washington, D.C.: Development Alternatives Inc. (February).

Louv, Richard (1983) America II: The Book that Captures Americans in the Act of Creating the Future, New York: Penguin Books.

Mushi, Mugumorhagerwa (1982) "African Governments and Indigenous Industrial Entrepreneurship: The Cases of Kenya and Ivory Coast," paper presented at the African Studies Association Meeting in Washington, D.C. (November).

126

Naisbitt, John   (1982) Megatrends, New York: Warner Books.

Ndongko, Wilfred (1984)   "The Political Economy of Development in Cameroon: Relations Between the State, Indigenous Businessmen, and Foreign Investors," paper presented at the Johns Hopkins (SAIS), Washington, D.C., (April).

Schumacher, E.F. (1973) Small is Beautiful: Economics as if People Mattered, New York: Harper & Row.

The Wall Street Journal, "A Special Report: Small Business," May 20, 1985.

Toffler, Alvin   (1981) The Third Wave, New York: Bantam Books.

_____ (1983) Previews and Premises,   New York: Bantam Books.

127

Official Documents and Reports

AID   (1984) The President's Task Force on International Private
       Enterprise: Report to the President, accompanied by a second
       volume, The Private Enterprise Guidebook. (December)

___   (1982) Policy Paper on Private Enterprise Development, and
       Policy Paper on the Bureau for Private Enterprise.

___   (1981) The Pisces Studies: Assisting the Smallest Economic
       Activities of the Urban Poor, edited by Michael Farbman of
       the Office of Urban Developent, Bureau for Science and
       Technology.

Anderson, Dennis (1982) Small Industry in Developing Countries:
       Some Issues, World Bank Staff Working Paper No. 518.

Page, John M, Jr. (1979) Small Enterprises in African
       Development: A Survey, World Bank Staff Working Paper
       No. 363.

Small Business Administration (1985) The State of Small Bus-
       iness: A Report of the President, transmitted to the Cong-
       ress (May).

World Bank (1978) Employment and Development of Small Enter-
       prises: Sector Policy Paper, (main author, David Gordon).

_____ (1983) Economic Development and the Private
       Sector; articles prepared for Finance Development, the quar-
       terly publication of the IMF and the World Bank.